CW01391095

Praise for *Strategy and Sustainability*

"If it's not *safe*, it's not sustainable. If it's not *sustainable*, it has no future. For those who understand the laws of successful industry, putting these practices into action is the foundation for a successful business."
— Mark Cutifani, Chief Executive, Anglo American plc

"*Strategy and Sustainability* reads very well and the blend of facts, views, and historical and technical data is a source of continuous inspiration. The recognition that perceptions and realities are highly influenced by regional and developmental factors makes the book very insightful."
— José Lopez, Former Executive Vice President for Worldwide Operations, Nestlé, Member of the Executive Committee, World Business Council for Sustainable Development

"Sustainability is a central dimension of good corporate governance. Mike Rosenberg's book provides an excellent framework and real cases on how senior executives and board members should include sustainability in strategic discussions."
— Jordi Canals, Dean, IESE Business School

"*Strategy and Sustainability* provides an excellent overview of the sustainability discussion, its development, and its relevance for businesses. It illustrates the different perspectives from senior management and environmental groups, helps to identify relevant issues, and assess strategic options. Accompanied by real business examples, Mike Rosenberg's book provides a holistic and good read about the different challenges to bridge the gap between the traditional business perspective and stakeholder expectations."
— Uwe Bergmann, Director Sustainability Management, Henkel

"Mike Rosenberg's encyclopaedic description of the issues that must be overcome in making environmental sustainability an important business priority - ranging from time horizon to point of view about the role of regulation and the priority of profits – nicely accomplishes his objective for the book: helping business and its critics to understand each other's perspective so that a feasible, implementable set of actions can be taken to ensure the long-term future of the earth."
— Jeffrey Pfeffer, Thomas D. Dee II Professor of Organizational Behavior, Graduate School of Business, Stanford University *and author of Power: Why Some People Have It—and Others Don't*

"Mike Rosenberg makes a persuasive argument that business success is incomplete without a dedication to environmental sustainability. Rosenberg suggests all leaders have a responsibility to be accountable on this important scale and offers concrete ways to make change for the better."

– Steve Capus, Executive Producer of the "CBS Evening News with
Scott Pelley"; Executive Editor of CBS News

"*Strategy and Sustainability* proposes that environmental sustainability is now a board-level issue, and that it is critical to business performance for both the risks and opportunities presented by a changing regulatory and consumer environment. Mike Rosenberg does this in plain English and without being judgmental, and in doing so, sets itself above so many pages of self-absorbed jargon that bewilder business readers trying to understand such critical issue."

– Randall Krantz, Founder, Constellate Global; Former Director of the
Sustainability Initiative of the World Economic Forum

"Mike Rosenberg's new primer on the corporate sustainability landscape nicely fills the knowledge gap for board-level business people. And almost anyone can use the thoughtful frameworks to better diagnose today's challenges and plan a more concrete and less risky path forward."

– "Hutch" Hutchinson, Senior Fellow, Rocky Mountain Institute;
former Director, The Boston Consulting Group

A Hard-Nosed and
Clear-Eyed Approach
to Environmental
Sustainability for Business

Strategy and Sustainability

Mike Rosenberg
Assistant Professor of Strategic Management,
IESE Business School, Spain

palgrave
macmillan

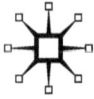

© Mike Rosenberg 2015

All rights reserved. No reproduction, copy or transmission of this publication may be made without written permission.

No portion of this publication may be reproduced, copied or transmitted save with written permission or in accordance with the provisions of the Copyright, Designs and Patents Act 1988, or under the terms of any licence permitting limited copying issued by the Copyright Licensing Agency, Saffron House, 6–10 Kirby Street, London EC1N 8TS.

Any person who does any unauthorized act in relation to this publication may be liable to criminal prosecution and civil claims for damages.

The author has asserted his right to be identified as the author of this work in accordance with the Copyright, Designs and Patents Act 1988.

First published 2015 by
PALGRAVE MACMILLAN

Palgrave Macmillan in the UK is an imprint of Macmillan Publishers Limited, registered in England, company number 785998, of Houndmills, Basingstoke, Hampshire RG21 6XS.

Palgrave Macmillan in the US is a division of St Martin's Press LLC, 175 Fifth Avenue, New York, NY 10010.

Palgrave Macmillan is the global academic imprint of the above companies and has companies and representatives throughout the world.

Palgrave® and Macmillan® are registered trademarks in the United States, the United Kingdom, Europe and other countries.

ISBN 978–1–137–50173–8 hardback

This book is printed on paper suitable for recycling and made from fully managed and sustained forest sources. Logging, pulping and manufacturing processes are expected to conform to the environmental regulations of the country of origin.

A catalogue record for this book is available from the British Library.

Library of Congress Cataloging-in-Publication Data
Rosenberg, Mike (Economist)
Strategy and sustainability: a hard-nosed and clear-eyed approach to environmental sustainability for business / Mike Rosenberg.
pages cm
Includes index.
Summary: "Business and environmental sustainability are not natural bedfellows. Business is about making money. Sustainability is about protecting the planet and the life forms on it. Business is measured in months, and quarters. Climate change, deforestation, and the reduction in biodiversity occur over decades or even centuries. Business is about maximising this year's profit. Sustainability often requires significant short-term costs to secure a very long-term benefit. It's difficult to bridge the gap. Strategy and Sustainability encourages its readers to move beyond the hype and takes a decidedly pro-business, fact based point of view, recognizing the complexity of the issues at hand and the strategic choices businesses can make. It blends the work of some of the leading academic thinkers in the field with practical examples from a variety of business sectors and geographies and offers a roadmap with which Sr. Management might think about engaging with the topic, not to save the planet but to fulfil its medium- and long-term responsibility to shareholders and other stakeholders"—Provided by publisher.
ISBN 978–1–137–50173–8 (hardback)
1. Entrepreneurship. 2. Sustainable development. 3. Strategic planning.
4. Environmentalism. I. Title.
HB615.R657 2015
658.4'083—dc23   2015029074

Typeset by MPS Limited, Chennai, India.

To my family, friends, and colleagues for supporting me, helping me find the time and space to think and write, and for sharing their ideas with me.

Contents

List of Figures, Tables, and Boxes / viii

Introduction / 1

1   **The Logic of Business: Governance and the Environment** / 6

2   **Modes of Response** / 41

3   **Strategic Issues** / 64

4   **Strategic Options** / 86

5   **Environmental Interest Groups** / 112

6   **Industry Examples** / 133

7   **Regional Differences** / 168

8   **What to Do?** / 199

Notes / 218

Index / 224

List of Figures, Tables, and Boxes

Figures

1.1 Prototype of the Clock of the Long Now ⁄ 22

3.1 Elements of a License to Operate ⁄ 67

3.2 Kano Diagram ⁄ 77

4.1 Compliance and Sensibility ⁄ 88

4.2 Strategic Options ⁄ 91

8.1 Framework for Strategic Analysis ⁄ 205

Tables

1.1 Six Fundamental Differences ⁄ 11

2.1 Summary of Lagadec's Differences
between Accidents and Crises ⁄ 49

5.1 Partial List of *Conservationist* Organizations ⁄ 120

5.2 Partial List of *Activist* Organizations ⁄ 123

5.3 Partial List of *Advocate* Organizations ⁄ 130

5.4 Types of Environmental Organizations ⁄ 131

Boxes

1.1 Different Approaches to Governance ╱ 8

1.2 Economics of Climate Change ╱ 16

1.3 Unilever and the Long View ╱ 20

1.4 Scenario Planning ╱ 23

1.5 Non-Market Strategy ╱ 37

3.1 Whole Foods ╱ 73

3.2 Noriaki Kano and Customer Satisfaction ╱ 76

6.1 Brent Spar ╱ 139

6.2 Electric Cars ╱ 144

6.3 Beverage Containers ╱ 151

7.1 The Arctic ╱ 197

Introduction

A little more than 50 years after the publication of Rachel Carson's *Silent Spring*,[1] concern for our natural environment has become widespread. It has gained an unprecedented legitimacy in civil society, been written into government regulation, and become standard business practice in countries such as the United States, Europe, and Japan, among others.

There is a segment of consumers who think about the environmental impact of what they do; routinely recycling glass, plastics, and paper and paying attention to the environmental reputation of the companies with whom they do business. In the West, we also take for granted landmark legislation largely enacted in the 1960s and 1970s, which protects air and water quality and regulates a number of aspects of the way business interacts with the natural environment.

Dealing with such regulations has become part of the job for management and many firms publish sustainability reports and have included environmental messaging in their marketing mix.

Despite all this progress, however, I believe that most CEOs and board members are disconnected from the environment and feel that, during difficult economic times, the issue is often pushed to the back burner if it is considered at all.

Business Schools, with some notable exceptions, may be part of the problem. Environmental sustainability is simply not considered in courses offered to board members and CEOs by the leading business schools and is normally taught as an elective to MBA students, if at all.

In my experience, most of the companies that place sustainability high on the agenda of senior management are those businesses that are directly connected to some of the key issues involved, such as oil and gas, water management, electricity generation, and other sectors.

This book has been written for the members of the board and the senior leadership team of organizations who have not focused their personal attention on environmental sustainability. Perhaps they have delegated the issue to competent managers in corporate affairs, legal, operations, marketing, and research & development. Perhaps they feel their firm is too small to engage with the issue or far enough away not to worry too much about it.

The reality, in my view, is that many business leaders have a hard time with the concept of environmental sustainability. For most, business is about making money. Sustainability is about protecting the planet and the creatures (including humans) on it. The time scale for many businesses is measured in quarters, annual results, and three- to five-year plans. Climate change, deforestation, reduction in biodiversity, and other impacts occur over decades or even centuries. It's difficult to bridge the gap.

One constituency that has the potential to help gain the attention of senior management is consumers. The problem is that, even in the relatively developed countries, it is difficult to get people to pay more for goods and services that are, in some way, supposed to be more sustainable. There does appear to be evidence of a growing segment of consumers who will, all things being equal, opt for the choice that they perceive to be more eco-friendly, but they appear to be reluctant to pay more money and difficult to pin down.

Strategy and Sustainability has been written to give board members and senior executives an introduction to environmental sustainability in order to determine what, if any, their personal involvement should be. The problem is that there is very little information and guidance available for such people, who up to now have found the topic distracting, idealistic, or possibly annoying. A balanced viewpoint is difficult to find in academia, or in many of the hundreds of books written on the topic.

In academia there is a deeply polarized situation. Most academic papers in this area are written by researchers and professors who care deeply about the environment and their personal bias shines through their research. Others are so highly skeptical that their work is not even taken into consideration by the first group. To make this all more complicated, the mathematical models needed to determine the environmental impact of any technology or practice are very complex and leave plenty of room for such bias to creep in via the assumptions one has to make in order to do the calculations.

In terms of the large number of books which seek to address business leadership, I find that many of them do not seem to understand how the men and women who actually build and lead businesses think, and thus get off on the wrong foot almost immediately.

In the first place, such books almost always start with the premise that Earth itself is in terrible danger. Although I, and most people I know in business, recognize the need to deal with local pollution and long-term climate change, the idea that the sky is falling seems a bit overstated. Second, many books which claim to be targeted at business people actually target business itself as the main culprit in creating the environmental challenges we face. Again I find this idea overstated and sensationalistic. Third, the recipes for developing more sustainable business models are often drawn from examples which may be hard for a typical manager or member of a board of directors to relate to, and thus impossible to put into practice.

Finally, and most importantly, such books tend to make some sort of moral appeal for business leaders to "do the right thing" without understanding that the primary ethical consideration for most people in business is to adequately perform their fiduciary responsibility to their firm and its shareholders, rather than do good for good's sake.

In my view, there is enormous potential to make radical improvements in the way we use natural resources and interact with the environment. Unlocking that potential is critical if we are to offer our current lifestyle to the 9 billion people who are projected to live on our planet in 2050.

These improvements, I believe, will not come about through onerous legislation but by business leading the way. The primary reason that business leaders will make this happen is not out of some moral commitment but in order to fulfill their commitments to their shareholders, employees, and customers.

The purpose of this book is thus to attempt to bring the worlds of business and sustainability a little bit closer. *Strategy and Sustainability* addresses business leaders and the board members in the language of business. It does not appeal to any moral concept of right and wrong but offers a range of responses that correspond to the particular circumstances of a specific company. The book strives to present a balanced point of view that looks at the issue based on sound business principles instead of hopeful assumptions and moralistic arguments.

The book will also prove useful to people passionate about sustainability, by helping them to better understand the issue from a business viewpoint and showing that a potentially effective way to influence the broader business community is to build profitable business models that are also sustainable.

Chapter 1 explores six fundamental differences between how, in my view, CEOs and board members think about their role in society and how environmental activists, lobbyists, journalists, and legislators think about the same ideas. The chapter will also show how the current interest in the environment is still quite new in historical terms and how senior management, at least in the United States, has been caught off guard over the last 60 years. Finally, the chapter will introduce the idea that environmental concern comes in waves and that each wave adds to the regulatory burden set on business.

Chapter 2 looks at how companies have been responding to environmental issues over the last 60 years. Six modes of response are discussed, which have much to do with each firm's governance structure and the interplay between the organization and environmental interest groups, the media, and governmental regulations that have developed over time.

Chapter 3 calls out the strategic issues in which environmental sustainability plays a key role, such as securing a license to operate, dealing with competition, and shaping consumer and societal perception.

Chapter 4 looks at the options open to business, which have to do with the degree to which companies choose to comply with legislation or go beyond compliance.

Part of the issue in choosing a strategy to deal with environmental issues is to fully understand environmental interest groups. Chapter 5 explores how the movement took off and outlines in broad terms who the main players are and how business might consider interacting with them.

Chapter 6 looks at five key industries: automotive, oil & gas, fast-moving consumer goods, mining, and IT/consumer electronics. The chapter has, as its starting point, the idea that, while there is some commonality across industrial sectors at the conceptual level, the specific issues facing one industry can be different from those facing another.

Many of the examples discussed in the book are drawn from the United States, because of the country's centrality to some of the issues at play and also due to my own experience and background. However, there are very important regional differences around the world. Chapter 7 focuses on those differences and contrasts the situation in the United States with that of Europe, China, India, and Africa.

Chapter 8 discusses my own framework for dealing with these issues. This involves understanding the firm's past and present, looking ahead with a 10–20-year time horizon; quantifying, to the degree possible, the cost and benefits of different options; and making sure that the entire organization – from the board of directors down to line management – understands the direction chosen.

Mike Rosenberg, Sitges (Barcelona), March, 2015

1

The Logic of Business: Governance and the Environment

Companies are run by people and, in my experience, the overwhelming majority of people want to do the right thing. The challenge is, of course, to figure out what the "right thing" is in a specific moment in time and when making a specific decision.

In 1966, Garret Hardin, a biology professor at the University of California, Santa Barbara, published an article titled "The Tragedy of the Commons,"[1] which went on to have an enormous impact on how people think about what is in fact the right thing to do in terms of the natural environment. Hardin wrote that "morality is system-sensitive," meaning that people are embedded in a specific context and that what might be considered proper behavior in one time and place, may be considered very differently in another.

In addition to the moral judgments of individuals, which depend on their upbringing, religious views, and place in society, companies also act in a contextual framework that guides the actions of the people in the organization.

Governance is the term that refers to how such decisions are made and who makes them.

In the private sector, firms are run by managers who typically report to some type of body or board of directors, which represents the interest of the owners of the company or some part of its shareholders. The structures and procedures that make up how these bodies are organized and interact with each other are commonly referred to as corporate governance. While the purpose of this book is not to focus on that issue – as this is done extremely well in a variety of other sources – an understanding of governance is critical in thinking about the way that companies interact with the natural environment, and is thus the starting place for this book.

Roles and Responsibilities

The exact relationship between a CEO and the board of a particular company depends on where it is based, the moment in the life of the organization, the industries and regions within which it operates, and the personalities of the people involved. It is, however, possible to generalize for the limited purpose of setting the stage for later discussion.

There is also numerous academic, legal, and practitioner-oriented material on this topic, which explores the nuances already mentioned. One such set of recommendations was made by a Task Force, put together by the Conference Board in 2013,[2] which talks about three key activities of a board.

In the first place while the "ultimate goals of a public corporation are to maximize shareholder value," the board should take all of a firm's stakeholders' interest into account so that value is sustainable over time. An organization is, of course, affected by the stakeholders around it, such as its customers and suppliers, and the communities in which it operates, but it also has an impact on its stakeholders. This issue of stakeholders and the relationship between a firm and those around it will be explored in more depth in Chapter 3.

The second task of the board is to manage itself such that it provides the proper oversight for the company and faithfully represents the interests of the shareholders as a whole. As part of their self-management, boards typically have a series of by-laws and committees that divide responsibility for key functions, such as audit, nominations, and so on.

Beyond this, the job of the board is to appoint and monitor the performance of the CEO, determine compensation for its members and the

CEO, assure that corporate accounts are in compliance with legislation, provide input to the company strategy, and manage critical mergers and acquisitions, which fundamentally affect the nature of the company itself. The board can also terminate the CEOs contract if, at some point in time, it feels that to do so would be in the company's best interest.

The CEO then has the role of appointing the management team of the company, managing the company on a day-to-day basis, and reporting back to the board at regular intervals.

Members of a firm's management team, such as vice presidents of different regions, functions, or business groups, often have an enormous influence on policy. However, the degree of their influence is dependent on the company culture, their particular function, level of expertise, relations with the CEO and the board, and even personality.

For that reason, this book focuses on the CEO and the members of the board and will refer to them as "senior management" understanding that the term might include a number of additional people in any specific company and that ownership structures and governance varies around the world (see Box 1.1).

BOX 1.1 DIFFERENT APPROACHES TO GOVERNANCE

There are very different approaches to corporate governance in different parts of the world and also very different structures in different industries and even in the same industries.

In the United States, the body representing the shareholders is called the board of directors and the most senior manager in the firm is called the chief executive officer (CEO). He or she answers to the board, which in turn has its own organizational structure such as the chairman and secretary.

Members of the board represent the shareholders who collectively own the company. In the United States and the United

Kingdom it is quite common for the firm to be widely held with thousands of shareholders with limited concentration of any particular person, company, or financial institution.

In 2007, the National Bureau of Economic Research published *A History of Corporate Governance around the World*,[3] which stresses the exceptional character of the widely held model.

In Germany, for example, the board is typically made up of the key senior managers of the company, but it, in turn, reports to a supervisory board in which the shareholders, union officials, and government also have representation.

In many countries, powerful families own or control much of the economy. In Asia and parts of Europe elaborate pyramid structures and cross holdings are used to give family-controlled investment companies a controlling interest in industrial firms, banks, and other types of companies, which then control still others.

In such firms the relationship between the family members and the professional managers who run specific businesses is very different than in a widely held firm where, in many cases, the CEO has a tremendous influence in the membership of the board and the direction of its deliberations and decisions.

Companies that are controlled by a particular family often have a parallel family council, which meets separately from the board but makes critical decisions about the long-term nature of family ownership and overall strategic direction of the firm. The Henkel family in Germany still owns 59 per cent of the ordinary shares with voting rights of their company and has insisted that Henkel's senior management make the firm's environmental performance a priority for the last 50 years.

In other countries large banks tend to own or have controlling interest in important parts of the economy and in a number of countries such as China, ownership of large firms is heavily intertwined with the government itself through state-owned enterprises, government banks, or companies owned by specific ministries such as the armed services. In some countries *much of the economy is owned by close associates, relatives of political leaders, or even, as in the case of Saudi Arabia, the royal family.*

Six Fundamental Differences

Many CEOs and board members appear to be a bit disengaged from the issues of environmental sustainability despite the tremendous progress that has been made over the past 60 years to raise awareness, legislate minimum levels of clean air and water, and develop a more accountable civil society.

In many companies, environmental compliance is an issue for corporate affairs, engineering, and operations teams and is about making sure the organization operates within the limits of the law. Large firms also engage lobbyists or participate in industry groups, which are involved in the public debate and work on shaping the legal environment itself.

Marketing concerns itself with looking at the degree to which consumers are interested in the issue and works with research & development (R&D) to come up with products that are, or are perceived to be, more environmentally friendly.

Finally, the corporate communications function is tasked with publishing annual sustainability reports. These show where the company is and how much progress it is making.

In this context, only those businesses that are directly connected to some of the key issues involved, or are "in the game"– such as energy exploration, water management, electricity production, and clean tech – have sustainability high on their strategic agenda.

The reason for this disconnect is that there are six critical differences between the fundamental logic of business and that of activists and legislators. These differences make it difficult for senior management to get their heads around the issues involved and/or make significant progress.

TABLE 1.1   Six Fundamental Differences

Challenge	Business Logic	Environmental Logic
1. Starting Point	Business has built the modern world and we owe our wellbeing to its incredible advances	The negative impacts of some businesses are unacceptable regardless of their importance
2. Time	With some exceptions, 3-5 years is a relevant planning horizon and many decisions are even shorter term	Pollution, and climate change will impact future generations and must be managed over decades or longer
3. Focus	A major focus of Senior Management is the financial health of the firm and its financial reporting obligations	Environmental issues can not be measured in economic terms as the issues are social, scientific and moral rather than economic
4. Risk	Risk is unavoidable and can be managed by evaluating its probability	Catastrophic risk is unacceptable and should be eliminated
5. Role of Government	The Government is the embodiment of the will of the people and sets the rules for business through the political process	The political process is heavily influenced by business and government and can not be trusted to protect the environment
6. Purpose	The purpose of business is to make money for its shareholders	The purpose of human activity is to be in harmony with the natural environment

Table 1.1 shows the six differences, which are explored in depth in the subsections that follow.

The purpose of calling out the differences is not to excuse senior management from looking at the environment, or even to challenge the basic logic and assumptions from which the differences spring, but to encourage a deeper understanding of them. Bringing about this deeper understanding is key to moving forward and is, to a large degree, the overall purpose of this book.

The starting point

The starting point for most business people is the belief that business is a force for good in the world and that our modern society has been created by the entrepreneurs and companies that built it. This basic belief in the power of business is well exemplified in the novels of Ayn Rand and the business legends from different times who have built our modern world.

For many, the industrial revolution was the jumping-off point for our modern way of life and James Watt's improvement to Thomas Newcomen's steam engine was a critical first step in building our modern world. Industrialization went hand in hand with the production of energy, electric lights, steel, railways, and the increasing opening up of the world.

Industrialists such as Carnegie, Rockefeller, Vanderbilt, Huntington, and so on are, in this world view, heroes as well as robber barons who built the world with their vision, money, hard work, and perhaps ruthless business practices.

Henry Ford is probably one of the most pivotal examples. Ford and his firm not only made tremendous strides in developing automotive technology and industrial processes to produce cars, but also raised wages and built a partnership with the labor force that would last to the current day.

In later years, Bill Hewlett and David Packard were considered to be heroes who, after studying radio science under Professor Frederick Termin at Stanford, went on to build HP. They also started what has become Silicon Valley, where generation after generation of entrepreneurs are able to raise capital to build the next wave of products and services of the digital age we currently enjoy.

In India, people such as Lakshmi Mittal and Ratan Tata hold a similar place in the country's business imagination, having built very large international businesses employing tens of thousands of people. Similar figures exist in virtually every country around the world.

At the heart of *the starting point* is the idea that we owe much of our material wellbeing to business leaders and the companies and industries that they have built. The homes we live in, the food we eat, the clothes we wear, the cars we drive, and the electricity, gas, and oil that power everything have all been created by modern industry over the last 100 years or so. The general feeling is that, as a result of industrialization and advancement, we live longer, healthier, and happier lives.

While all of this might seem obvious to business people, it may not be so clear to others. Having grown up with the comforts of the 21st century, average people in the developed world forget about the 19th century and do not even look to the developing world where many of the basic goods and services we consider normal, such as access to clean water and sanitation, simply do not exist for everyone.

Instead, there is a contrarian view that business is somehow bad and that its focus on profits is done at the cost of the environment or the people who work in its mines, factories, distribution networks, and stores. While business leaders might find this post-industrialist view fundamentally naive, it is, in any case, the starting point for many environmentalists.

A more reasonable starting point for the discussion is to recognize the tremendously important role that business plays in society and to high-light the responsibility that business has for any negative environmental impacts directly or indirectly caused by its activities.

The starting point is so important because the vast majority of senior executives in any company have a deep belief in what the company is doing; meaning they often have a very difficult time discussing or read-ing about the views of those who reject the very reason for that firm's existence.

While not all managers in tobacco companies, for example, are smokers, practically all of them believe in people's right to smoke and feel their industry is being unfairly attacked by the anti-smoking lobby who, in their view, want to build a "nanny state" where the government will tell us what we can and can not do.

Digging into the facts, it appears that in many countries cigarette taxes actually make up a significant portion of the disposable funds of the state. There is often political give and take between the finance ministries of these countries, which rely on tobacco revenue and the health minis-tries, which are doing their best to eradicate smoking.

What is even more fascinating is the cognitive distance between execu-tives in the tobacco business and people who are stridently anti-smoking.

Between these two groups there can be no middle ground or compromise simply because the activists look for the complete destruction of the industry and will not engage in any serious discussion about the importance of the tobacco crop to farmers, cigarettes to the small shops that sell them, and the negative impact of the illicit trade in cigarettes. Anti-tobacco activists stress the negative health impacts of smoking and call attention to the deliberate misinformation efforts on the part of tobacco companies in the past as proof of corporate malfeasance.

In *Atlas Shrugged*,[4] Ayn Rand's character, Dagny Taggart, is a smoker. She sees the act of harnessing fire for our personal enjoyment as a fundamentally transcendent act, because it demonstrates mankind's ability to use our ingenuity and will to build the world around us. This, I believe, is *the starting point* for most men and women in business.

Time

The second basic assumption that affects the way the men and women who run companies think about the environment is their concept of time. While there are exceptions (discussed further), the logic of business leads managers to think in the relatively short term. At its longest the time frame is typically three, five, or perhaps ten years into the future.

While business measures time in years, the people focused on environmental issues, such as scientists, academics, politicians, and political activists, look at trends that occur over decades and even centuries. This difference in the understanding of time and planning horizons is central to the challenge of bringing business strategy and sustainability closer together, and thus will be explored in detail.

The point of view of business people stems from the idea of the time value of money, the strategic planning process in many firms, the complexity of the business environment, individual career planning, and the kind of human motivations that drive people who choose a career in business in the first place. The following section will look into each of these ideas and finally deal with notable exceptions.

Time value of money

One of the cornerstones of business logic is the time value of money. Simply put, a given amount of money has a different value today than it will have tomorrow, because one could put the money aside and invest it at some interest rate that will make it grow. The same logic also applies to future earnings or cash flows, which can be discounted back to the present day so that they can be compared to other investment opportunities.

There are two key points in doing an analysis of discounted cash flow. The first is to estimate the actual amounts of cash flow over time based on market growth, share, and the evolution of prices and costs as well as net changes to working capital including inventories, payables, and receivables. The second is to choose the appropriate discount rate based on the weighted average cost of capital of the enterprise plus an additional amount for risk or the degree of confidence placed in the estimations discussed already. The higher the uncertainty, the higher the discount rate.

In many business decisions, a discount rate of 10–15 per cent can be considered normal. What is important for this discussion is that the present value of any future cash flow drops off very quickly after the first five or ten years of a new investment or activity. The value of $100 in ten years, for example, is less than $40 at 10 per cent and less than $25 at 15 per cent.

The impact of the time value of money can not be understated, because the financial implications of virtually any decision are looked at very closely. Also, due to the way the mathematics are calculated, the near term is simply more important than what happens far into the future.

This is the logic that brings the controversial Danish economist Bjorn Lomborg to conclude that the cost of attempting to slow the pace of climate change is simply not worth the money and that the world and its population would be better off with a different set of near-term priorities (see Box 1.2). There is, of course, more to a business decision than its financial implications, but finance is the language of business and does have an important influence.

BOX 1.2   ECONOMICS OF CLIMATE CHANGE

Bjorn Lomborg is a Danish economist who is a controversial figure in the discussion about climate change. He is the author of 12 books, including The Skeptical Environmentalist, Cool it, *and* How to Spend $75 Billion to Make the World a Better Place.

Lomborg has spent the last 15 years trying to convince anyone who will listen that focusing on climate change mitigation is an enormous mistake. The essence of the argument is that implementing the Kyoto accords or any subsequent climate program will cost tens of billions of dollars and that the money would be better spent on other things such as water, sanitation, and childhood nutrition.

At its present level of economic development, for example, a 1 meter rise in sea levels would devastate Bangladesh and displace tens of millions. The Zeeland region of the Netherlands is, on the other hand, already below sea level and the Dutch have no problem maintaining the system of dykes because they are well off.

Lomborg argues that the challenge is to bring prosperity and new technology to the world and that the net present value of adaptation such as constructing dykes in 50 years is negligible. From his economic point of view, it is much cheaper to fix the problem later on and focus on more urgent issues today.

To drive home this idea Lomborg organized a meeting of former Nobel Prize winners in 2004, which was called the Copenhagen Consensus and has brought together a similar group every four years since. The group determines that fighting climate change is a relatively low priority compared to other problems when looked at from a cost–benefit perspective.

While one could argue with Lomborg's ideas and call into question the idea of assigning economic costs and benefits to social issues, what is remarkable is the vehement antagonism which is directed at his central thesis and the man himself. There is even a small cottage industry of anti-Lomborg pundits who dedicate enormous time and energy to prove him wrong on every point.

Strategic planning

A second issue driving the time horizon in business is the strategic planning process that most large firms undertake on an annual basis. While this topic is well covered elsewhere,[5] such processes typically deal with three time periods.

First, there is the short-term planning cycle, which often deals with the next 12–18 months and is closely tied to the firm's budget, financial plan, and management objectives such as sales, production, headcount, and other targets.

Second, most firms have a medium-term component to the plan, which deals with looking two to five years out and is done in broader brush strokes dealing with competitive position over time, penetration of new markets, and issues having to do with the structural transformation of the firm, which normally takes longer than one year.

Many firms are, for example, in the process of implementing shared service centers in relatively low cost countries around the world. This process takes time to get the information systems in place, hire and train new staff, and then move processes one by one to the new centers, eventually realizing cost savings. Such programs will typically find mention in both the short-term and immediate-term components of the strategic plan.

Finally, many planning processes have a separate space for long-term considerations and often define the long term as being between five and ten years. Few firms have developed rigorous processes for developing long-term plans, although there are exceptions, which will be discussed further.

Complexity

A third issue, affecting senior managers, is the need to focus time and attention on certain critical issues in the context of a complete overload of information and complexity.

Increasingly managers are operating in a matrix environment where multiple interests are competing for attention across different product lines and geographies. Reporting to a CEO will be global directors of product groups; regional directors for major parts of the world such as Europe, North and South America, Asia Pacific, the Middle East, and Africa; global functional heads for finance, purchasing, operations, human resources, and perhaps others; and, in some cases, global customer groups. The complexity this creates can be overwhelming.

CEOs increasingly spend their time shuttling between performance reviews, financial presentations, and very high-level discussions with shareholders in order to keep investors informed and the share price buoyant. Much of the remaining time is absorbed by working with key members of the management team who, in turn, are also increasingly bogged down – or as one senior manager called it, "snowed under."

These basic trends are made more complex by the emerging 24/7 email culture where everyone appears to be available all the time and individuals can only keep their sanity by constantly prioritizing the avalanche of information coming at them. This has led to a managerial world in which there is a strong dichotomy between two extremes. On one side we have regular events such as performance reviews and board meetings, which can not be postponed or re-scheduled as there are simply too many people involved or "moving parts" to coordinate. On the other extreme we have the crisis of the moment, which has to do with operational or people issues and needs management attention immediately. Time for careful contemplation of complex issues is very hard to find as the agenda

of senior management is limited to what is required by the formal planning process and financial calendar on the one hand, and the crisis of the
moment on the other.

Career planning

A fourth issue, which drives senior managers to think about the next
three to five years rather than a longer time period, is their career cycles
and those of their colleagues. The fact is that many executives will
change jobs within three to five years in any case, either by moving to a
new position in their current firm or perhaps by accepting an opportunity
at a different firm.

IESE Business School's Paddy Miller even developed a theory based on
his observations of executives at HP's printer division in Barcelona. The
basic idea of what Miller calls Mission Critical Leadership is that in today's
hyper-connected and fast-paced business environment, a general manager should only be in a specific role for about 1,000 days or just under
three years.[6]

The danger is that there is always a temptation to improve short-term
results at the expense of long-term capabilities. Cutting R&D expenditures, for example, will have an immediately positive impact on EBITDA
or net profit, but may have a very negative impact on the company further down the road.

At issue is that even while most managers resist that trap, it is very difficult to argue for lower short-term financial performance, because one
needs to make large investments, which will only bear fruit long after
everyone involved has moved on to new challenges.

Human motivation

Professor Miller's 1,000-day model, discussed earlier, reflects a certain
managerial outlook that is very common in the men and women who
come to IESE programs and events. It is a mindset that is deeply focused
on the immediate task and making things work. This also tends to

shorten the time horizon of the individual's thinking in terms of what can be controlled and is therefore most relevant.

During workshops in which managers are asked to develop scenarios for the world, as well as their region and industry, with a 20-year time frame, it is striking to observe how difficult it is for most of them to think so far ahead. People in business generally like to deal within clear bounds of certainty. Disruptive events or black swans[7] are simply not considered as part of everyday decision making and it takes a tremendous amount of energy to get most managers to think beyond the event horizon of the normal and expected. Writing about World War I, for example, Harvard's Niall Ferguson found that traders in London's financial markets were behaving on the assumption of "business as usual" literally days before the onset of war![8]

On the other side of this motivational issue is the very human desire to build things that last and leave a legacy for the future. Certainly this idea holds true in many family-owned businesses around the world and, as already mentioned, there are exceptions to relatively short-term thinking in business.

Notable exceptions

Many men and women in senior management positions do take a longer view in their thinking and decision making. Unilever's CEO, Paul Polman, for example, has stopped giving quarterly reports to the market and insists on a ten-year time horizon[9] (see Box 1.3).

BOX 1.3 UNILEVER AND THE LONG VIEW

Working together with the Canadian Pension Plan's Investment Board, McKinsey & Company's senior partner, Dominic Barton, launched an initiative in 2013 called Focusing Capital on the

Long Term, which is about getting boards of directors to reverse the trend toward short-term thinking.

Paul Polman

Unilever's Paul Polman is a member of the initiative who stopped giving quarterly guidance to the financial press, which has changed the nature of the company's shareholders by attracting the kind of capital that allows it to set bold, long-term, financial, and sustainability goals. He also changed Unilever's internal compensation system to make sure his management team was focused on the ten-year goal of doubling the firm's turnover and making it more sustainable.

Polman began his career at Proctor & Gamble, and has also served in an executive capacity at Nestlé, and became CEO of Unilever in 2009. He says that "thinking in the long term has removed enormous shackles from our organization" and that "better decisions are being made."[10]

Polman is also chairman of the World Business Council for Sustainable Development, is a member of the International Business Council of the World Economic Forum, and serves on the Board of the UN Global Compact and the Global Consumer Goods Forum

The Clock of the Long Now

An even more extreme example of long-term thinking is the construction of a 10,000-year mechanical clock, which is being financed by Jeff Bezos, Brian Eno, and many others, in a mountain in Texas. The purpose of the project and associated foundation is "to provide a counterpoint to today's accelerating culture and help make long-term thinking more common."[11]

While a time frame of 10,000 years might be a bit long for most people, part of the answer in bringing the worlds of business and the environment a bit closer will be to expand the time horizon of business so that more comprehensive tradeoff discussions and risk assessments can be made.

FIGURE 1.1 / Prototype of the Clock of the Long Now

Besides particular leaders such as Polman, exceptions often result from the specifics of certain industries, national culture, and the industrial fabric of certain countries, or all three factors together. In terms of industries, there are businesses where the planning cycle for major investment must be made over long periods of time despite the time value of money discussed already. A nuclear power plant, for example, has a very high capital cost, which can only be amortized over the full life of the investment. Similarly, investments in oil exploration and production, shipbuilding, aerospace, and other key strategic sectors are made on a long-term basis.

Perhaps the best example of a company building long-term thinking into its managerial culture is Royal Dutch Shell. The organization routinely uses scenario planning to think about what will happen in the future and to analyze potential investment options. The problem with scenario planning is that it is very time consuming and technically difficult to do well (see Box 1.4).

BOX 1.4 SCENARIO PLANNING

Scenario planning has its roots in military strategy, with its use in business largely credited to Pierre Wack and his team at Shell. Back in the 1960s, Wack and his group developed a scenario for the future supply and demand for crude oil, indicating that there would be a shortage of supply in the mid 1970s due to the confluence of a number of disparate factors including rig counts, shipping capacity, refinery capacity, and other issues.

While the scenario was reportedly considered unlikely, Shell nevertheless took steps to prepare for it and equipped its new refineries in Europe so that they could process heavier crude oil from Nigeria just in case. When the countries belonging to the Organization of Arab Petroleum Exporting Countries put in place an embargo on shipments to the United States, Canada, Japan, the Netherlands, and the United Kingdom in October 1973, Shell was one of the only major oil companies with a plan B in place.

Since then Shell has continued to invest in producing very thoughtful and complete scenarios for the future, which are published on its web site but also used for its long-term strategic planning. Major projects are expected to show their relevance and potential profitability not only in the most likely or desirable future but across a range of possibilities.

What scenario planners do is to develop a list of trends that will shape the future or "drivers" and then to work out different combinations of how they may play out. These are normally collapsed into two or three broad scenarios, which are internally consistent but fundamentally different.

> *The time horizon for a scenario exercise depends on the nature of the company for which the scenarios are being developed but can be 10 or 20 years, or even longer.*
>
> *In short workshops looking 20 years into the future conducted at IESE Business School, managers from different industries typically consider drivers such as the growth of the economies of China and India, the price and availability of oil and gas, developments in computers and communications technology, and the impact of climate change.*
>
> *The essence of scenario planning is the recognition that forecasting typically does not uncover sweeping changes to the status quo and that it is basically impossible to predict the future with any certainty.*
>
> *What is possible, and actually tremendously useful, is to imagine different futures and then to think through a company's typical options in light of those futures.*

In terms of countries, Japanese and Chinese business managers appear to take a longer-term perspective, because of cultural traits.[12] However, the long-term nature of Japanese and Chinese companies also has to do with the industrial and financial structure of both countries. Japanese companies are often owned by networks of other firms organized into federations or *Kereitsu*, and that system is thus safeguarded, to some degree, from the quarterly pressure that is felt by public corporations in the United States. A large number of Chinese companies are backed either directly or indirectly by the Chinese government, which appears to have its own long-term goals.

Focus

A third difference between the logic of business and that of the environment is the importance of financial considerations. As already stated, the language of business is finance and, as one moves up the hierarchy in modern corporations, the weight of financial issues becomes larger and larger, while the more operational issues of customers, products, and supply chains receives less attention.

Initiatives such as the United Nation's Global Compact in 2000 have led a number of firms to publicly embrace the idea of the triple bottom line. Many organizations now publish regular reports on sustainability and on progress in the environmental area as part of those reports.

While these reports have made a huge difference in the level of transparency in many companies and have had an important impact on operations, it does not appear that their publication has shifted the focus of attention of senior management as much as the hype would have us think.

While this point may not be politically correct, the fact is that most of the time and energy of the senior management of publicly traded companies, and even many privately held ones, is focused on managing the financial fundamentals of the company they serve and there are several reasons for this.

One is that increasing the value of the firm is, in many ways, the primary responsibility of senior management. As Charlie LaMantia, former CEO of Arthur D. Little, used to say, the acronym CEO stands for the three responsibilities of the office: customers, employees, and owners. The owners of the company are its shareholders and the value of their investment is reflected in the share price. While stock markets go up and down for a number of reasons, the most closely managed are the financials, which are read and commented upon by professional analysts and the financial press. Thus a focus on financials and the share price is more than understandable, and in fact part of the fiduciary responsibility of senior management and the board.

At the board level, legislation such as the Sarbanes-Oxley Act in the United States has placed even more responsibility on the board to be fully aware of the ins and outs of a firm's financial statements. In some cases this has taken over the board's agenda and squeezed out more strategic issues, such as the company's response to long-term trends and new technological and market developments.

In order to align management with the interests of shareholders, CEOs and other executives are often given share options, which become financially significant to the degree that the company's share price appreciates over time. This, in turn, gives them "skin in the game" and a personal motivation to increase the value of the company.

A final, and compelling, reason to focus on the financials and a company's share price is that a CEO's tenure will most likely be cut short if the share price drops significantly on "their watch." Even board members will see their own reputation damaged if they oversee a deterioration of a firm's position.

This focus on the financial aspects of operations lies in contrast to the focus of special interests and non-government organizations (NGOs) who are passionate about protecting different aspects of the environment. The mindset here is that a monetary value can not be placed on the preservation of the natural environment or the wellbeing of people and that even to do such calculations is, to some extent, immoral.

Risk

The fourth difference has to do with risk. According to the director of public affairs for an international consumer products company, the fundamental activity of business is risk management. Risk and reward are at the heart of every business decision and managers are trained at business schools to deal with both the quantifiable and qualitative aspects of risk on a regular basis.

Philosopher Roger Scruton rallies against government officials and activists who believe that certain risks are simply unacceptable and thus should be removed from the realm of possibility.[13] The fact is that many industrial processes routinely use materials that are harmful to people and the natural environment, but the end products and services that are eventually produced are desirable. Gasoline, for example, has an outstanding energy density and has allowed us to build our homes where we want and enjoy a degree of personal mobility never imagined in the not so distant past.

Oil exploration and production and the refining and distribution of gasoline is a technologically and managerially complex business, which uses highly toxic chemical processes and, of course, poses risks to the men and women who work in the industry as well as the general public.

There are, therefore, a number of processes in place to manage the overlapping phases in the supply chain and take care to minimize accidents. From a business viewpoint, the issue is how to manage risks in a cost effective way. There is an entire service industry devoted to developing acceptable standards for a wide variety of processes and installations and ensuring that those standards are met.

Companies such as DNV GL and Lloyds, among others, are constantly perfecting their understanding of risk mechanisms. They work with their clients to find ways to reduce the risk of industrial accidents, and alongside the insurance industry that covers such unlikely events.

On the other side of the debate, however, are those who believe profoundly that certain risks should simply not be considered. Nuclear power plants provide an example of what many people believe is the answer to both our future energy needs and climate change. Others feel these plants should be taken off the table as an option, because of the possibility of devastating accidents.

On this issue of risk, there is again a fundamental difference between people involved in business and those who are concerned about the environment. As for the latter group, no amount of analysis or contingency planning can be acceptable for risks they feel should not be taken.

There are also risks which can not be evaluated and quantified using our current level of science and mathematics, because they have to do with little-understood phenomena or simple unknowns. Climate change is an area that some business people fit into this category – there are simply too many factors at play for us to be certain about what will happen in the next 50–100 years. The vast majority of scientists do, however, insist that we already know enough about climate change to justify taking action on the problem on a planetary scale.

On this type of issue it is common to refer to the precautionary principal, which essentially states that if there is a possibility that a practice or compound can cause catastrophic harm, then its use should be halted until we can be sure that it is safe. At the Rio summit in 1992, the idea was formulated as follows:

> *where there are threats of serious or irreversible damage, lack of full scientific certainty shall not be used as a reason for postponing cost-effective measures to prevent environmental degradation.*

From a business viewpoint, the precautionary principal can be seen as blocking innovation, as it puts the burden of proof on the innovator to demonstrate that the innovation not only does no harm but will never do so. Scruton feels the whole idea to be unscientific at best and possibly ridiculous.[14]

Role of government

A fifth issue, which separates business people from environmentalists, is their basic assumption about the role of government in regulating commerce and the common good.

In "The Tragedy of the Commons,"[15] Hardin uses the example of population control to argue that government coercion is necessary to get people to use common resources responsibly. Hardin maintains that there will always be people who place their self interest above that of the community and that other people who voluntarily curb their behavior will feel taken advantage of. Thus the best approach is to establish some sort of coercive mechanism by which the public good is applied to all involved.

Since its publication, Hardin's article has stirred much debate and controversy. There are many examples that show he is essentially correct, and numerous others of communities and industries that have effectively regulated themselves. Business people are largely sympathetic to Hardin's central idea that some coercion is necessary, but tend to have a nuanced view toward government regulation with at least three components.

In the first place, business people generally look to government to set the rules of commerce and to make a "level playing field" where all competitors behave according to those rules. At the same time, however, senior managers often have a profoundly skeptical view of the efficacy of most government regulation and hence believe strongly that the rules should be limited to the minimum necessary. The idea is reminiscent of the description of the ideal referee in a soccer match as one who blows the whistle at the start of the match and then swallows it.

Finally, it is a widespread view among business people that it is a legitimate part of the public political process for business to actively engage with policymakers. Organizations do their best to have the rules written in a way that is favorable to the company or industry involved.

The logical end point for many people in business is thus that their primary responsibility is to comply with the law in whatever country or region they operate in. Harvard's Forest Reinhardt, however, asks when a firm should go "beyond compliance."[16] While this question will be explored in depth in Chapter 3, the framing of the issue here shows the fundamental assumption at play.

This view is quite different from that of many environmental groups and, to some degree, the general public who look at the issue in a different yet complex way. Firstly, people feel that companies should "do the right thing" regardless of the current legislation or cost. Secondly, there is a tendency on the part of people involved with environmental issues to feel that more government legislation is better than less. Finally, there is also a level of mistrust and skepticism regarding the relationship between business and government in many countries. In some parts of the world, the issue is the role of professional lobbyists and campaign contributions in the political process, whereas in others it is more about explicit or illicit financial connections between government and business.

Purpose

Of all of the differences discussed in this chapter, perhaps the most basic and profound is that of purpose. As discussed in the section entitled *The starting point*, men and women in business generally believe strongly in what they do. They understand that the purpose of business is to make a positive return for shareholders and, for a variety of reasons, choose to work in a specific industry or company.

Typically managers usually have some basic affinity for the product or service in question or have, over time, come to enjoy what they do. Many people in the automotive industry, for example, love cars and trucks; people working in different media businesses normally have a deep passion for storytelling. Additionally, most people also believe that there is some degree of transcendental importance in their work and that by making steel, building homes, or developing new drugs they are making the world a better place or improving people's lives.

Beyond an individual's choice of industry and company is a more basic desire to provide for the material wellbeing of themselves and their family. Since the first step is to believe in the purpose of the business itself, achieving economic success on a personal level is a logical and added bonus.

This basic understanding of purpose contrasts sharply with that of many people engaged in the environmental debate who draw their own energy and commitment from what they perceive as fighting against clear and present dangers to our natural habitat. The conflict between these two definitions of purpose can not be understated and it is important to get past them if real progress is to be made on almost any issue.

At the risk of caricaturizing, for the activists, business leaders are uncaring plutocrats who only think of themselves at the cost of the natural environment. On the other hand, business leaders may feel that some activists and media professionals are not adding value to the world and only pushing specific issues in order to raise awareness so that they can fund their own organizations, sell newspapers, and so on. Only when both sides begin to understand and respect the other is it possible to make serious progress.

Caught Off Guard

Up until the industrial revolution, the natural environment dominated man and commerce. People rose and went to sleep largely based on the movements of the sun and wealth was deeply tied to the land.

In the period leading up to 1900, the world saw miracle upon miracle of modern ingenuity: Steam ships and railroads reduced transport times and the telephone and telegraph linked the world as it had never been connected before. Authors such as Charles Dickens chronicled the times they lived in, showing the human tragedy of the period and bringing to life the intensity of the environmental impact of the industrial revolution.

What has gotten lost in our day and age is, however, how recent this past is in historical terms and how far some parts of the world have, in fact, advanced. What is key to understanding the current situation of the world is that the spread of electrification, and access to water and sanitation, has been uneven and, while many of us live in what has been called a post-industrial society, much of the planet is still struggling to catch up.

The purpose of this section is thus to provide some context to the debate about business and the environment, and to show how organizations have been, to a large degree, caught off guard by the issue during the last 60 years.

The discussion here focuses primarily on the United States and, to a lesser extent, on the United Kingdom, although similar developments occurred in parallel in other parts of the world. Chapter 7 will highlight differences between the United States and other regions including Europe, China, Africa, and India.

The rise of conservation

While industrialization was changing the face of the world during the second half of the 1800s a parallel and in some ways symbiotic conservationist movement was steadily gaining ground in the United States and the United Kingdom. Inspired by philosophers such as Ralph Waldo Emerson, writers, including Henry David Thoreau, were talking about man losing touch with nature in the headlong rush toward industry.

Thanks in large part to pressure from this movement, the U.S. Congress passed landmark legislation in 1864 protecting the giant Sequoia trees in the Yosemite valley in California. In 1871, the country's first National park was declared in Yellowstone, Wyoming. Immediately after, in 1872, conservation writer John Muir led a group of San Francisco naturalists – The Sierra Club – in lobbying the government to expand the protection in Yosemite and make a second national park.

The national parks superseded local and even state authority to protect large tracts of land under direct federal supervision. Local interests were, more often than not, focused on the immediate benefits of jobs and industry rather than the less tangible benefits of conservation and environmental protection.

It was at this time that a hero of the Spanish American war and avid outdoorsman, Theodore Roosevelt, entered politics as governor of the State of New York. He went on to become Vice President to Republican William McKinley and ascended to the Presidency after McKinley's assassination in 1901. Besides pushing back against powerful industrialists and starting the Panama Canal, Roosevelt also created a lasting environmental legacy. He expanded the national park system, creating five additional parks and pushing through the Antiquities Act in 1906, which allowed his administration to proclaim 105 sites, such as Devils Tower Wyoming and part of the Grand Canyon, as national monuments.

> *I recognize the right and duty of this generation to develop and use the nature resources of our land; but I do not recognize the right to waste them, or to rob, by wasteful use, the generations that come after us.*[17]

The United Kingdom followed a similar path, passing legislation to protect wild birds in 1872, ancient monuments in 1882, and the foundation of the National Trust in 1895, which is today the largest landowner in the United Kingdom.

Two world wars

World War I was the first major conflict in which all of the new technologies could be harnessed for the purpose of war, with horrific results. Massive artillery bombardments, the indiscriminate use of mustard gas, and the importance of oil-powered mechanization on land, at sea, and in the air characterized the war and accelerated industrialization.

As the war grew to a stalemate in Europe, industrial mobilization, and the eventual entry into the conflict of the United States with its own manufacturing base, finally tilted the balance in favor of the Entente.

Even more industrialized than World War I was World War II, which saw the development of strategies and tactics specifically developed to make the best use of industrial technology, such as the mechanization of tanks, the militarization of early rockets, and aerial bombardment. This war, of course, ended with the most impressive and frightening technological achievement so far in history, that is, the atomic bomb attacks on Hiroshima and Nagasaki in August 1945. With 120,000 immediate deaths and the destruction of both cities and the natural environment around them, the atomic bomb exemplified our domination of the natural world.

The last 60 years

After World War II much of Europe and Japan had to be rebuilt and the world entered into a period of unprecedented economic growth taking advantage of advances in chemical engineering, metallurgy, electronics, and other technologies fueled largely by oil and coal.

Between 1950 and 1970, the global economy took off as millions of people's lives were changed by electrification, household appliances, and the modern distribution of consumer products. The economic boom also had an enormous impact on the natural environment and established a pattern that has, over the last 60 years, had a cumulative impact on business.

One of the first major environmental issues was about what were called "killer fogs." In 1948, about 20 people died in Donora Pennsylvania when pollution from two U.S. steel plants was caught in an unusual temperature inversion on Halloween night. A similar event happened in Poza Rica, Mexico killing 22 people in 1950. Just two years later, 4,000 people died over a four-day period in London in 1952, hundreds perished in New York City in 1953, and another 1,000 lost their lives in Los Angeles in 1956.

Scientists found that pollution combined with atmospheric fog produces what came to be called smog (smoke + fog) and, depending on the type of pollution, could cause different levels of harm to people. These events led to the passage of landmark legislation such as the Air Pollution Control Act (1955) in the United States and the Clean Air Act in the United Kingdom (1956).

The 1950s were also noted for the first public reactions to the testing of nuclear weapons and the discovery of Minimata disease, or mercury poisoning, caused by the negligence of the Chisso Chemical Company in Japan. Jacques Cousteau also fired up people's imagination with his 1953 book and subsequent award winning documentary *The Silent World*. This combination of public awareness and the discovery of real environmental problems led to what has been called the first wave of environmental activism in the 1960s.

In 1962, Rachel Carson, a marine biologist and nature writer with the U.S. government, published *Silent Spring*. In the book, Carson documented how DDT, a revolutionary insecticide that was credited with eradicating malaria in the West, posed a threat to entire ecosystems and could build up over time in humans and animals, potentially causing cancer.[18] Carson's book provoked a strong reaction from the chemical industry but her research led to a ban on DDT. More importantly, she changed the public's attitude toward the relationship between our everyday practices and the natural world around us.

The late 1960s was also a time of social change in the United States and Europe. The anti-war movement, together with new music and lifestyle choices, brought 100,000 young people to San Francisco in the summer of 1967 (The Summer of Love), massive student strikes in Paris in 1968, and a peace march, which turned into a riot, in Trafalgar Square in London. The hippie and anti-war movements joined forces with the early environmentalists for Earth Day in 1970. The so called "teach in" involved 20 million people and was supported by environmentalists, hippies, and U.S. Senator, Gaylord Nelson. The early 1970s went on to witness the U.N. Stockholm declaration, the founding of the Environmental Protection Agency and the National Oceanographic and Atmospheric Administration in the United States, and the publication of *The Limits to Growth*[19] by a group of business leaders and scientists called The Club of Rome. The result of all of this activity was the passage of new environmental legislation around the world, which built the basic environmental protections that are in place in the West today.

The 1970s are also remembered for what the U.S. Environmental Protection Agency (EPA) calls "one of the most appalling environmental tragedies in American history" – in Love Canal, New York. The site had been used as a chemical waste dump in the 1920s in line with the environmental legalization of the times. In 1953, the Hooker Chemical Company covered the canal with earth and sold it to the city of Niagra Falls for $1 with the warning not to use the land. Some years later a school and housing project were built on top of the site and it was not until the late 1970s that horrifically high levels of miscarriages and birth defects were discovered amongst the families living there.

In terms of the relationship between business and the environment, the most striking aspect of this example is the idea that a company can be liable to pay damages and cleanup sites that were contaminated long ago and were, at the time, legal. Hooker Chemical was purchased by Occidental Petroleum in 1968 and when the situation at Love Canal became clear, Occidental was required by the EPA to pay the $129 million cost of cleaning up the site and relocating the families.

The 1980s were marked by several large-scale environmental disasters, including the gas escape at Union Carbide's plant in Bhopal, India, the nuclear power accident at Chernobyl, and an explosion at a Sandoz facility near Basel, Switzerland, which turned the river Rhine red and killed countless eels and fish downstream of the site.

The decade also saw steady progress on other fronts such as the delimitation of a class of chemical refrigerants collectively called chlorofluorocarbons (CFCs) and a ban on exporting toxic waste from one country to another with less stringent environmental controls. One of the biggest issues in the 1980s was the so called "hole in the sky" or depletion of the ozone layer, which was found to have been caused in part by CFCs. DuPont had first commercialized CFCs in the 1930s but also took a leading role in developing a commercially viable alternative. The result was the Montreal Protocol, signed in 1987, which essentially phased out CFCs worldwide.

By the 1990s the focus had begun to shift from environmental protection to climate change. This stemmed from increasing evidence that carbon concentrations were rising in the Earth's atmosphere, most likely due to the burning of fossil fuels to heat our homes, power our society, and drive our cars, trucks, and airplanes. This interest eventually resulted in the Rio Declaration and the Kyoto Protocol, which were signed by the governments of most countries (excluding the United States) in 1997, and the publication of the first and second reports of the Intergovernmental Panel on Climate Change (IPCC).

Catching the Wave

John Elkington, an early environmental practitioner and author, makes the point in *Cannibals with Forks*[20] that interest in the environment has come in a series of waves. If we look at the brief historical review given in this chapter, we can see these waves in action, although it appears that they started well before the 1960s, which Elkington refers to as the first wave.

One could call the late 1800s one such wave, in which the progressive political movement coincided with a passion for the outdoors by conservationists such as John Muir, adventurers, and big game hunters such as Teddy Roosevelt.

During the late 1950s and 1960s the accidents mentioned already created another wave of environmental concern. This popular worry, combined with the anti-war movement and the appearance of the hippies in Earth Day in 1970, led to the founding of Greenpeace and like-minded groups.

A third wave appeared in the late 1980s and was widely focused on climate change and carbon concentration as the principal culprit. That wave appeared to crest in the 1990s with the 1992 Rio meeting and subsequent Kyoto accords.

At the time of his writing in 1999, Elkington suggested that a new wave was starting to build. However, it appears that the bursting of the dot com bubble in 2001 delayed the trend until it too seemed to peak with the boom of investment into so called clean tech just before the 2009 financial crisis.

Looking at the rise of environmentalism as a series of waves has a number of implications for business strategy. Firstly, the waves appear to have a pattern that is consistent with Baron's non-market strategy model (see Box 1.5). Tragedies or events occur that provoke public outrage. Interest groups and the news media amplify people's concerns and when the support of solutions become broad enough, political leaders step in either by choice or against their will. Eventually legislation is developed to curtail specific practices or encourage others. Finally, an institution is tasked with implementing and/or enforcing the legislation.

BOX 1.5 NON-MARKET STRATEGY

In 1995, Stanford's David Baron introduced the idea of non-market strategy, which he later went on to develop in his landmark textbook, Business and its Environment.[21] The essence of the idea is that, to be successful, business should not only develop its market strategy using frameworks such as Michael Porter's 5 forces or Arnaldo Hax's Delta Model, but also needs to take into account other trends that affect society and give rise to government regulation, such as that of environmental sustainability.

Baron's framework is conveniently built around four words starting with the letter I. The first one, of which sustainability is a broad example, is Issues. Issues are ideas that catch the attention of some part of society and can place constraints on or give opportunity to business.

Issues include the fight to save the giant sequoias in the late 1800s, air and water pollution, nuclear safety, climate change, and a wide range of other topics.

The next part of the framework is Interests and this includes all types of non-governmental actors who have been or may become involved in a particular issue. One important group of interests are the news media and another are the NGOs such as the Sierra Club, Greenpeace, and others that have formed over the years to work on addressing one issue or group of related issues.

Institutions are the government departments or ministries that have the mandate to regulate certain aspects of civil society and these can be local, regional, national, and transnational in nature. In the United States, for example, the Environmental Protection Agency is an important institution for many issues connected with the environment.

The final part of Baron's framework has to do with the Information that is developed and disseminated in the public and private discourse around a specific issue. One of the themes that will be developed further is that, on many issues connected to the environment, the level of scientific data and mathematical modeling needed to shed light on some issues is quite complex.

Due to this complexity, information can easily be misunderstood, manipulated, or misrepresented by interests pushing one side or the other of almost any debate.

Typically, at some point there is a national crisis or the economy takes a downward turn which takes the issue out of the public eye until the next cycle. What is critically important from a business point of view, however, is that even after a set of issues drop out of public view, their institutional momentum continues and each wave adds regulations to those that came before setting the bar for compliance higher every time.

Part of that momentum comes from a portion of the young men and women who were involved in the protests going on to pursue careers in politics or public administration. As these people enter public life they slowly and steadily support some of the ideas they embraced as students and activists. This phenomena has been called the "long march through the institutions of power" by German communist Rudi Dutschke, who would eventually join the green movement in Germany.

As will be developed in Chapter 8, one of the first tasks for a firm's senior leadership team is, therefore, to understand where the environmental impacts of the company's activities are in terms of this evolutionary perspective. This will enable the management team to anticipate subsequent waves of public interest and administrative regulation.

Conclusion

The purpose of this chapter has been to re-frame the central challenge of putting together the worlds of business strategy and environmental sustainability in terms of the way senior management tends to look at the world. The chapter highlighted six differences between what could be called a business viewpoint and that of activists, journalists, and legislators. Looking at the six differences shows how business, at least in the United States, has, over the last 60 years, been caught off guard by many aspects of the environmental movement.

Firstly, business has a hard time engaging with groups which do not share *the starting point* and reject the idea that business is a positive force in the world.

Secondly, the time frames that interest groups and government regulators who are concerned about the environment use are simply well beyond the scope, planning cycle, or even the imagination of many people in business.

Thirdly, a tremendous amount of senior management's time and energy is spent on looking at financial issues. Unintended environmental problems can occur below the radar or even as a result of cost saving measures that had sound business logic but for which environmental externalities were not foreseen or considered.

Fourth, business is about dealing with a certain degree of risk and when accidents happen business leaders are often taken aback that people affected by the accident simply reject the idea of probabilistic risk and immediately look to malfeasance or criminal neglect as the root cause.

Fifth, at the limit, business leaders look to governments to establish the rules of the game and are often surprised when the public or activists demand that they comply with some higher law. The idea, for example, that a firm is liable for actions done many years ago, which were legal at the time, can be considered unfair by business people who want the rules to be clear.

Finally, business leaders often have a hard time understanding people who question the very reason for the existence of the companies in which they serve. This is especially true for entrepreneurs, who may feel their purpose in life is deeply tied to the firm they have built and thus any rejection of the organization is a rejection of themselves. Taken together, these basic differences explain why so much of the history of business and the environment, as discussed in this chapter, involves surprise, crisis, and catch up.

The purpose of starting with corporate governance and the six differences is that only by addressing the fundamental logic of business can one hope to engage in any kind of sensible discussion about how business strategy can be reconciled with environmental sustainability, which is the purpose of this book. In terms of corporate governance, the fiduciary responsibility of the CEO and board members is to protect the value of a company and increase that value over time. To do that, it is important not to be caught off guard or surprised, as has happened in the past. When that happens, senior management respond in a number of ways, which are explored in Chapter 2.

Modes of Response

Over the last 60 years, issues connected to the environmental impact of business have come up in each wave of environmental awareness discussed in Chapter 1. The following discussion looks at how firms have responded to these issues and explores some high-profile and well documented cases from the past.

While there are a myriad of ways in which different companies around the world have responded to environmental issues as they came up, it is possible to group those responses into six broad categories which will be discussed in this chapter. It is important to note that the modes of response are not set out in terms of good and bad but rather in terms of the environmental engagement of senior management, as the purpose is not to criticize past behavior but to look at it clearly in the hope of gaining insight for the future.

A first level of response by many firms is refusal to accept that a problem exists, because to do so would be to call into question the basic idea of what a company, or even an industry, is all about. This reaction is called *denial*.

A different response is when an organization, or specific people in that organization, are aware of environmental externalities but take deliberate action not to inform the general public or other stakeholders and even deliberately attempt to confuse the issue. The term *cover up* is used for this type of response, despite its negative connotations, and could be further broken down into additional categories exploring levels of ethical conduct and possible malfeasance.

The phrase *crisis management* is used to describe what happens when a firm is faced with catastrophic environmental impact. In this case, a higher level of preparation and awareness of environmental issues may make it easier for an organization to weather the storm.

The term *environmental PR* describes the activities of those firms that have made an effort to put the best positive spin on their activities to reduce or control the ecological impact of their operations; although perhaps not truly engaging in substantial reflection or re-design of their products, services, or operations.

Engagement is used to describe those organizations making efforts to understand and work with the issues involved in environmental sustainability. The distinction between *engagement* and *environmental PR* has to do with the breadth, and depth, of the response to environmental issues by senior management.

The final mode of response is referred to as *transformation and renewal* and this is reserved for those firms that, for whatever reasons, have chosen to fully embrace the challenges posed by environmental problems and turn them into opportunities by re-inventing the firm itself.

As mentioned earlier, there is no direct correlation between good and bad, as those are moralistic judgments and the purpose of this chapter is descriptive, not prescriptive. Also, different people will interpret the different examples from their own moral perspective and they were chosen to illustrate the modes of response rather than question the motives of the people involved.

Denial

Denial is a well known psychological response to loss or pain and essentially allows humans to continue to function in the face of what is perceived as catastrophic loss, heartbreak, or worry. Typically, the issue is not a question of lack of data. Rather the person who is "in denial" simply chooses, at a basic level of their consciousness, to "tune out" the data that does not fit into the picture of reality that they need, for a variety of reasons, to believe in.

The important aspect of *denial* in the context of the environment is that there is no malfeasance involved. An entrepreneur who has invested his or her life in building a business might genuinely be incapable of seeing a problem that can threaten its very existence. When data emerges that shows there might be a problem, it becomes very difficult for that person to spend time, attention, and money on it.

The pattern that has emerged over and over again in the last 60 years is that a given industry or industrial practice has some environmental side effect, or externality as it is called, about which the leadership of the companies involved are unaware.

Average people are often the first ones to notice irregularities or problems. They then might get the attention of journalists or other groups who have a specific interest in the subject at hand. At some point the story is picked up by the media, confronting the leadership of a company or an industry with a problem they did not foresee or expect. Their initial reaction is often one of *denial*.

A complex and even controversial example of what could be considered denial is the response of the chemical industry to charges made in the 1950s that industrial pesticides in general, and dichlorodiphenyltrichloroethane (DDT) in particular, may have an adverse impact on the environment. These charges were brought to a head with the publication of Rachel Carson's book, *Silent Spring*, in 1962.[1] As briefly discussed in Chapter 1, Carson – a marine biologist and nature writer for the U.S. government – and her book are credited with inspiring much of the environmental movement and the response by many firms was simply to not engage in the debate, because they saw the claims being made by Carson as far-fetched or too impractical to consider.

To properly understand the story of DDT it is important to go back to the context of the times. The allies had recently emerged victorious in World

War II and part of the credit for that victory was given to science and engineering, which had made tremendous strides during the war and in the period immediately after it.

DDT was first synthesized by Paul Muller, a Swiss chemist, in 1939 in France and was found to be the most powerful insecticide ever seen. It turned out to be instrumental in saving the lives of thousands of allied soldiers by wiping out lice that were responsible for a typhoid epidemic and then became the "weapon of choice" in the widely successful fight against malaria in the late 1940s and 1950s.[2] DDT was so successful that Muller was awarded the Nobel Prize for physiology in 1949 and production soared from zero to 82 million kilograms by 1962.

In *Silent Spring*, Carson documented the way that DDT had a negative effect on the larger ecosystems in which spraying was occurring. The book became a media sensation and CBS news Special Reports ran a segment on it.

Silent Spring was based on a series of articles that came out in *The New Yorker*, and even before its publication the book provoked a strong reaction from the chemical industry. The heart of Carson's message was that minute traces of DDT had been found far from target spraying areas and that it and other compounds were being used indiscriminately without fully studying their long-term effects on birds or people. She was, in effect, employing what would come to be called the precautionary principal mentioned earlier.

Carson wrote:

> it is not my contention that chemical insecticides may never be used. I do contend that we have put poisonous and biologically potent chemicals indiscriminately into the hands of persons largely or wholly ignorant of their potentials for harm.[3]

At times the response of the chemical companies was to find alternative scientific experts such as American Cyanamid's Robert White-Stephens to contest the claims. At other times the response was that fully understanding long-term effects would take too long and cost too much money and that without DDT and other pesticides we could not feed the world and fight tropical disease such as Malaria.[4]

Eventually U.S. President John F. Kennedy would commission a study into the matter and, after a long political and legal process, DDT and another seven pesticides that Carson focused on were eventually banned in the United States.

Fifty years later, the debate about DDT continues and there is even a web site called Rachel Was Wrong, which is supported by a free market, limited government group called the Competitive Enterprise Institute. At the heart of the message of this and other groups with a similar agenda is the contention that the dangers Carson was concerned about have not come about and that, meanwhile, the fight against malaria and other tropical diseases has faltered.

While one could question the motives of groups on different sides of the issue today, it seems that in the late 1950s and early 1960s there was a serious disconnect in the minds of the chemical industry people who truly believed in what they were doing and simply had a hard time understanding how a nature writer with limited data could get the attention of the media and the President of the United States.

The idea that their miracle product, which was increasing food yields and saving lives, could potentially do harm was simply not part of their thinking and their initial response was similar to the psychological state of denial. Dr. White-Stephens speaks with conviction on the CBS program when he says that Carson's assertions were "gross distortions of the actual fact" and "unsupported by scientific evidence." While perhaps closed minded, the response to *Silent Spring* does not seem to be the result of a dark conspiracy of the chemical companies trying to deliberately poison the general public.

A very different situation exists when senior management recognize that there is a serious problem and take steps to hide the problem and/or distract public and official attention from its cause.

Cover Up

The key difference between a firm denying to the world and themselves that their activities have resulted in harm to people, animals, or the natural environment and covering up such damage is that, in the case of *cover up*, the executives realize what is going on but make a business decision to manage the situation and to "keep it quiet." Whether such behavior is morally correct, or even legal, is an important question that is very capably dealt with in the literature on business ethics. The fact is that, regardless of anyone's personal opinion about such behavior, it has happened in the past and will likely do so in the future.

Echoing a point mentioned in Chapter 1, most people try and do the right thing. Thus, even when the collateral effects of air or water pollution are horrific, it is unlikely that those effects were caused on purpose. What is far more likely is that these kinds of impacts were initially not understood or were unexpected. The question then becomes: Why would executives involved in such an activity try to hide the impacts once their full or partial extent is clear?

On one level, a *cover up* might occur because there are considerable costs associated with full disclosure, which might include financial expense, the loss of jobs and reputation, and possibly even criminal prosecution. Avoiding those costs can be seen as a benefit.

In addition to this kind of cost–benefit thinking however there are also psychological processes in play that may push the people involved to cover things up. One such process is referred to as *prospect theory*. According to *prospect theory,* people tend to be more risk averse when looking at potentially positive outcomes and actually take on more risk when trying to avoid loss.

In the case of unintended industrial harm, the additional costs of acknowledging a problem might be avoided if a cover up is successful. The problem is that the overall risk of exposure will be greater, and the penalties worse if found out. If one applies *prospect theory* to the situation, the people involved may choose to *cover up* the event despite the possible consequences, like a gambler who keeps betting on a losing streak.

Another psychological process involved is the idea of *group think* and individuals not wanting to lose contact with some larger group to which they belong, such as their colleagues in a company or industrial partners. According to psychologist Mark Levine, people may go beyond their own moral compass to protect the reputation of a group to which they feel particularly attached in order to protect its reputation.

A significant case of a possible *cover up* happened in Donora Pennsylvania in the period following the worst case of industrial air pollution in U.S. history, which was briefly mentioned in Chapter 1. U.S. Steel had two units operating in Donora one of them was operating smelters to produce zinc and the other making wire. The zinc plant in particular produced toxic levels of fluoride gas. It seems that while residents had been complaining for years about the impact of the plant's emissions on their health, property, and the surrounding vegetation, the company had always maintained that everything was safe while at the same time settling the odd lawsuit out of court.

On Halloween night in 1948 the valley experienced a temperature inversion and a thick fog settled on the town trapping the emissions from the plant, killing 20 people, and affecting the health of thousands more. What followed was an official investigation that papered over the incident and resulted in an out of court settlement for the class action lawsuit that was brought by 130 residents against the company.

A pollution expert who studied the incident, Phillip Stadler, reportedly found high levels of fluoride in victims of the incident.[5] The same source found that the industry also had its own data showing the connection between fluoride gas and the fatalities, which was suppressed. The official government report indicated that "bad weather and a mixture of pollutants" were to blame and fluoride was not singled out.

At the time of the accident, fluoride was important to the U.S. nuclear weapons program as well as the aluminum, steel, and phosphate industries. At the same time, a campaign was in place to add fluoride to the water supply to fight tooth decay. Some critics of drinking water fluoridation contend that the plan was actually to dispose of large quantities of fluoride and to "launder" the chemical's image in the eyes of the public.[6]

U.S. Steel never admitted responsibility for the disaster or released its own analysis of the air taken at the time. It did shut down the zinc plant soon after the incident and eventually closed the wire mill.

To be clear, there is no direct evidence of senior management of U.S. Steel or any of its managers participating in an active *cover up* in the case of Donora. The case is used as an example because of its importance in the history of the relationship between business and the environment and the possibility that a *cover up* might have happened.

The president of American Steel & Wire, the unit that operated the plants, was Clifford Hood, who would continue with the company and eventually succeed Benjamin Fairless, the president of U.S. Steel at the time of the incident.

In November 1946, *Life Magazine* published a photograph of the board of directors of U.S. Steel and called them "possibly the most powerful group of men in the whole industrialized world." On the board were the chairman of J.P. Morgan and other bankers, a former governor of New York, presidents of other industrial firms, a number of lifelong U.S. Steel executives, and the U.S. envoy to the Vatican.

While it is unthinkable that this group would deliberately poison thousands of people, one could imagine them or some smaller group of managers farther down the chain of command discussing the need to pay off the victims and keep the incident as quiet as possible while ordering the shutdown of the facility.

While the example of Donora is inconclusive, the question of how to prevent lower levels of a firm from covering up or presenting misleading explanations of environmental problems when under pressure is an important one. For that, the only answer seems to be to develop a deeply accountable culture within a firm so that information will actually flow to the top if it needs to. One company that had developed such a culture was, in fact, Union Carbide, which will be discussed further.

Crisis Management

Patrick Lagadec is one of the world's foremost experts in managing very complex crises who distinguishes an accident from a crisis[7] and makes the point that the way an organization deals with a crisis will reflect its culture and the character of the people involved.

Lagadec suggests five broad phases of crisis management,[8] which will be used in this section to look at the Bhopal disaster in 1984 based on an account of the company's response written by Jackson Browning, Union Carbide's former vice president for health, safety, and environmental programs.[9] In his account, Browning underscores several of the elements described by Lagadec and credits Carbide's response to the tragedy for the firm's ability to survive the event.

TABLE 2.1   Summary of Lagadec's Differences between Accidents and Crises

Accident	Crisis
Well-defined failure with statistical probability	Unexpected or unimagined occurrence
Known effects are contained and immediate, although potentially tragic	Immediate effects are serious and long-term consequences possibly worse
Well-defined steps are taken and the situation controlled	Response is ad hoc at best and met with enormous and unexpected difficulties
Press releases and communication are straightforward	Communication with stakeholders and the press is exceedingly complex
Insurance coverage is clear	Insurance is ill defined and litigation likely
Little uncertainty	Paralyzing uncertainty
Timing of key steps is predictable	Critical phase(s) can extend over a long and uncertain time frame
Limited group of people involved	Extraordinary numbers of people involved

Union Carbide's headquarters in Danbury Connecticut is ten and a half hours behind Bhopal in central India. The gas escape, which killed several thousand people outright and may have resulted in tens of thousands of deaths, happened in the early morning of December 3 in Bhopal and word gradually reached managers in the United States, who had their first formal meeting at 6:00 AM, which was by now 4:30 PM in India.

Anticipating

In terms of anticipation, Carbide was well known for being a very safety conscious company and had developed a strong company culture, which maximized safe operations around the world. While Carbide had emergency plans in place, the scale of the accident was in Browning's words "overwhelming."

Such an occurrence had never been anticipated by the management team at the plant or Carbide management and the fact that a densely populated town had grown around the plant after its opening had not been explicitly considered.

One of the issues that occur during a crisis is that large numbers of people from different organizations become involved and that trust is not only key in the fast-paced, uncertain environment but also very difficult to achieve on the go. It is therefore essential that a broad coalition of stakeholders already be engaged with each other prior to the onset of a full blown crisis. Getting an organization to reach beyond its boundaries, and even discuss unthinkable challenges such as systemic failure, requires courageous leadership.

Detecting

Detection of the scope of the incident was made difficult by the lack of telephone lines to the small town of Bhopal. Carbide executives in the United States were being updated by BBC news reports taped and played back over the phones from its offices in New Delhi and Mumbai.

A major crisis might require management to react to relatively weak or conflicting signals and break with long established paradigms about what kind of information is considered valid. Lagadec points out that information flow actually slows down or even stops in a crisis and that leadership is needed to create a culture of vigilance that will actually listen to signals from unconventional sources.

Reacting

Part of Carbide's response was to immediately shut down another plant making the same products in the United States until it could identify the cause of the gas leak. Carbide's chairman, Warren Anderson, took charge of a special task force, publicly assumed moral responsibility for the incident, and flew to India with a medical and technical team in order to assist the victims and stabilize the situation at the plant.

What Carbide had not anticipated was the reaction of the Indian government, which placed Anderson under house arrest upon his arrival and blocked access to the plant and the victims. The company was deeply surprised by the degree of hostility and mistrust that met their efforts to help the victims and control the plant despite 50 years of working in the country and the fact that Carbide had an Indian partner in the venture and the management team were Indian nationals.

When dealing with risks that are off the scale an organization can be shut down by anxiety and the temptation to "wait and see" or fall into denial. Again, strong leadership is required to act even before everything is clear but to avoid over reaction and to keep everyone within and even outside of the organization on the same page.

Inventing

What Lagadec calls "collective creativity" is needed to deal with contradicting demands and to break through deadlock obstructions, and cynicism. For this to happen it may be necessary to create a "fundamental rupture" with the management systems normally in place and constantly assess what is happening on the ground.

Eventually, Carbide managed to persuade the Indians to allow them to neutralize the remaining methyl isocyanate at the plant and a year later to give them access to the data they needed to determine the cause of the incident. With the data, Carbide found that the gas leak was the result of sabotage by a disgruntled employee who had deliberately put water into a storage tank of methyl isocyanate producing the cloud of deadly gas. This finding has, however, never been accepted by the Indian government.[10]

Mobilizing

A final point to draw out from the Bhopal incident is the effort that was needed to build open and regular communications with the press, Carbide's own people, and other interested parties. Of particular concern was that for months Carbide simply did not know what had happened in the plant. While mobilization of resources within and outside of the organization can be critical to success, the problem is that many managers and public servants are normally not trained for living with high degrees of uncertainty, and thus the selection of the men and women involved in managing a crisis is critical. Browning showers praise on the people of Carbide, such as the technical team leader and public relations staff whose "versatility" and "stamina" were significant assets in this case.

The two conclusions that come from this brief discussion of crisis management are the need to develop a corporate culture that is resilient enough to survive such a crisis – as it seems increasingly likely that they will happen sooner or later – and the urgent need to prepare the senior management team for their role when the time comes.

After calmly ditching his Airbus A320 in the Hudson River in January 2009 and safely evacuating 155 passengers and crew, Captain C.B. "Sully" Sullenberger claimed that it was his deep training and regular simulator experience that guided him on how to react. The question is how much training and simulator time are CEOs, board members, and other key executives spending on crisis management? Is there a collective understanding about systemic threats to the business and what to do if the unlikely or unexpected does occur?

During the last 60 years few companies have developed this level of preparation for crisis and, in many cases, the response to large-scale environmental problems has been to respond with better or worse versions of *crisis management*.

Environmental PR

Over the last 60 years there has been an unprecedented increase in awareness and transparency of the environmental footprint of businesses in many parts of the industrialized and developing world. Some of the new openness is due to regulatory requirements and some due to voluntary reporting such as the triple bottom line, which encourages firms to publish their social and environmental impact on an annual basis in addition to their financial results.

According to the Global Reporting Initiative, which develops guidelines for producing such reports, there were 2,500 companies in their database at the end of 2012 and publishing a sustainability report "is now standard practice for the majority of the largest companies in the world."[11]

Sustainability reports are generally published by professional managers in the corporate communications department. Firms spend significant sums to generate such reports. An entire industry has actually sprouted up, led by the large auditing firms, to help companies calculate a number of parameters such as the carbon footprint of each facility.

In addition to regular reports, a number of firms around the world are increasingly incorporating messages about their commitment to sustainability and the activities they pursue into their broader communications strategy, which can include industrial and consumer marketing.

Activists often draw a distinction between the messaging done by firms that they perceive to be genuine and those simply paying lip service to the issue in their communications. This latter practice is often referred to as *greenwashing*, playing on the term *whitewash*, which is often used to describe a cover up or an attempt to distract attention from a problem.

EnviroMedia president, Kevin Tuerff, a pioneer in green marketing based in Austin, Texas defines greenwashing as:

> *when a company or organization spends more time and money claiming to be "green" through advertising and marketing than actually implementing business practices that minimize environmental impact.*[12]

The line between a company being transparent about its activities and engaging in a public relations campaign can be difficult to draw and is subject to one's own view about what should and should not be done and shared. In order to take the ethical issue out of the discussion, the term *environmental PR* is deliberately neutral and used to describe a wide set of responses regardless of motivation and level of commitment.

An interesting example of *environmental PR*, which has provoked a large degree of controversy and is even the subject of a Harvard Business School Case study,[13] is John Browne's tenure as CEO of BP. John Browne joined BP as an apprentice while still in school and stayed with the company for 30 years working in Exploration, Production, and Finance. He became group chief executive or CEO in 1995 and would guide BP during the next 11 years in three fundamental directions.

In the first place, Browne continued the work started by his predecessor David Simon to bring BP to competitive scale. Simon had acquired Standard Oil of Ohio in 1987 and Browne continued by first merging BP with Amoco in 1998, then ARCO in 2000, and starting TNK-BP in Russia.

Second, Browne completed Simon's massive cost reduction program and re-focusing efforts, reducing BP's headcount from 120,000 employees to 53,000. BP also flattened its corporate structure in an attempt to make the management team more accountable and performance driven.

Thirdly, Browne made an unprecedented commitment to the environment in a series of actions and investments leading in 2000 to the launch of the "Beyond Petroleum" campaign in an effort to re-brand the company.

In 1996, Browne broke ranks with other oil companies and left the Global Climate Coalition, which had been working in *denial* mode by trying to disprove the idea that carbon build up could cause global warming. Later, speaking at the Stanford Business School in May 1997, Browne made reference to the second report of the Intergovernmental Panel on Climate Change (IPCC) and said it is time to take action, "not because we can be certain climate change is happening, but because the possibility can't be ignored."

Under Browne's leadership, BP launched BP Solar, invested heavily in wind energy, put in place an internal BP carbon trading scheme, built on Amoco's strong history in the environmental area, and developed a comprehensive approach to corporate social responsibility (CSR) and transparency.

One area of concern at BP as it became larger and leaner was a series of accidents in the late 1990s and early 2000s leading to an explosion at its Texas City refinery in March 2005, which killed 15 people, and later the catastrophic failure of the Deepwater Horizon rig in 2011, which killed 19 and released an estimated 5 million barrels of oil into the Gulf of Mexico.[14]

Of course, John Browne had left BP five years before the Deepwater Horizon accident occurred, but one charge is that under his leadership a culture of results first and safety second was allowed to emerge and that BP's traditional culture of technical excellence was watered down and not brought to bear on assets acquired in the large mergers. Another is that the relatively small investments in solar and wind and the public stance on climate change were only public relations and that the real agenda was about building a larger, more profitable company.

The facts are that BP's solar business eventually grew to be a $200 million company, the company also installed about 2,600 MW of wind power, and did freeze its own emissions of greenhouse gases at roughly 1990 levels thanks to the initiatives launched by John Browne.

After Browne's departure, his successor, Tony Hayward, made a speech at Stanford insisting on the harsh realities of the energy business; he proceeded to unwind Browne's initiative closing BP Solar, selling off the wind investments and also reportedly scaling back his public relations team in the United States.

The tragedy of Hayward's tenure was that he did make safety his "top priority," but such cultural change takes many years and the mistakes that led to the tragedy in 2011 were made long before the accident. Lacking strong public relations, Hayward was harshly criticized for his response to the Deepwater Horizon incident, as will be discussed in Chapter 3, and ended up leaving BP in 2012.

Engagement

The next response that has been pursued by few companies in the past but that is becoming more and more common recently is referred to as *engagement.*

Engagement is used to describe a set of actions that clearly go beyond good communication and has both an internal and external component. Internally, companies become engaged when they look at the environmental footprint across the firm and take active steps to reduce that footprint. Externally, these types of firms typically also reach out and engage with a wide variety of stakeholders and also partner directly with environmental interest groups.

The line between what was called *environmental PR* in the previous section and *engagement* can be debated in a specific instance such as the example of John Browne and his tenure at BP discussed earlier. Some would say that BP was clearly engaged, while others would accuse it of only engaging in *environmental PR* or even greenwashing. Perhaps the best way to distinguish genuine *engagement* is to quote the U.S. Supreme Court Justice Potter Stewart whose definition of obscenity was "I know it when I see it."

One example of engagement is Toyota Motor Corporation and their commitment to alternative drive train technology for cars and light trucks. In 1992 Toyota adopted the Toyota Earth Charter and created an environmental committee, chaired by its president, to develop and then implement a series of four-year plans. At that time, Toyota stated that there was a need to reduce the environmental burden caused by cars, because it was the only way to protect its future core business, and placed the development of environmentally friendly technologies at the top of its corporate agenda.

Ever since then, Toyota has been pursuing the parallel development of electric vehicles, fuel cell electric vehicles, and hybrids. In 1997, Toyota followed Honda to launch a mass market, specially built vehicle with a hybrid power train, the Prius, which would go on to become the leading hybrid on the market and firmly establish Toyota as technology leader.

What is interesting about Toyota's efforts on hybrid technology is both that it is still being developed in parallel with other alternative power trains and that Toyota has led the industry in placing its hybrid synergy drive on a number of vehicles across its product range rather than limiting it to Prius.

One can also read about Toyota's commitment to the environment in the introduction to its annual reports in which Toyota's president has reiterated that commitment every year since 1992 and in its sustainability/ environmental reports, which have been published since 1999.

Another example of a company that seems to be genuinely engaged in environmental issues is Henkel, the German-based manufacturer of adhesives, home care, and beauty care products. Henkel's engagement with the environment goes back to 1953 when it established an ecology department that went beyond toxicology to start to look at the life cycle impact of its products. In 1981 Henkel included explicit commitments in its management principals stating "to aim for and achieve compatibility between production processes, products, and systems, on the one hand and the environment, on the other."

Henkel became one of the first international companies to publish an Environmental Report in 1992, which later evolved into its Sustainability Report and earmarked R&D funds to find substitutes for harmful chemicals in its detergents. Systems and audits were put into place to measure the group's environmental performance and in 2000 a sustainability council was set up with members drawn from senior management.

Henkel was also one of the first companies to sign the United Nation's Global Compact and in 2007 put in place a five part sustainability strategy, which set targets for improvements in energy, water, materials, health and safety, and social progress. In 2011 Henkel introduced its Factor 3 strategy, taking the idea one step further.

Factor 3, adds a performance dimension to the five areas mentioned here and commits Henkel to become three times more effective in its use of energy, water, and materials in terms of generating social impact, financial returns, and safety in the next 20 years.

Henkel's commitment has been led by members of the Henkel family who control the voting shares of the company and are embraced by management. Along the way Henkel has won numerous awards from different ecological interest groups and is ranked in the top tier by Bloomberg, and other sustainability indexes.

For Henkel managers, the sustainability strategy has lowered costs in energy, water, and materials, is an important motivational tool for its people, and has become a sales argument for the retailers who carry their products.

Henkel's CEO Kasper Rorsted is fully behind the new strategy and has rolled it out across the company. According to Rorsted:

> *Many companies have sustainability strategies and targets, but sustainability can only become an integral part of people's daily work if all employees understand the underlying principles.*[15]

What both the Toyota and the Henkel examples show is a corporate level commitment to engage with the environment. Elements of that *engagement* are that it is led visibly and actively by senior management, that programs are put in place with both a medium- and long-term perspective, and that the initiatives are undertaken with a clear connection to strategy and not as an add on or afterthought.

The next response goes even further than *engagement* and uses an environmental threat as an opportunity for *transformation and renewal* of the organization itself. Toyota, for example, never stopped making cars and light trucks; and while it has put more hybrids on the road than anyone else, it is still one of the world's top two manufacturers. Henkel, likewise, is still very much in the laundry detergent business and while it has made great strides to make the environmental impact of its products more benign, it is still part of the current paradigm.

Transformation and Renewal

Transformation and renewal has to do with a firm completely re-inventing a company's business model in light of changing circumstances in the environmental area and breaking out of conventional thinking. Over the last 60 years few organizations have undergone such sweeping transformation, although there are examples of firms apparently going in that direction and then falling short or even reversing course, as happened in BP.

One pattern is for companies to embrace a single aspect of environmental technology and to develop its business strategy around that. An example of this is Gamesa, a wind energy company based in Spain, which was founded in 1976 to develop industrial machinery and equipment for the automotive industry. Over the next 20 years Gamesa branched out into other areas such as robotics and aerospace. In 1994, Gamesa began making wind turbines under license from Vestas, the Danish company that still leads the sector. In 1995 Gamesa started developing its own wind farms and in 2001 the company went public and focused its activities almost exclusively on the wind energy business, where it now enjoys a global presence and is ranked number six in the world.

Another pattern is for firms to recognize the changing requirements of the industry they are in and undergo profound internal change to bring themselves in line with what they perceive to be the new reality. A relatively small but significant example of this pattern is the deep retrofit of the iconic Empire State Building in New York City.

Built in 1930 and once the tallest building in the world, the Empire State Building is famous for the 1933 movie, *King Kong,* and literally hundreds of other films in which it is used as a cultural reference point and landmark. In addition to its viewing platform and visitor's center it is also an operational office building with 2.7 million square feet (250,000 square meters) of space.

In 2009, the building's new owners, W&H Properties, joined with the Clinton Climate Initiative, Johnson Controls, and the Rocky Mountain Institute to begin a deep retrofit of the building to make it more attractive to top tier tenants. In addition to restoring the art deco lobby and bringing back its former glory, they also worked to make it energy efficient. The program replaced all 6,500 windows, put in modern insulation, added a state of the art controls system, and completely revamped the HVAC equipment. The results are millions of dollars of energy savings, independent certification putting the building in the top 10 per cent of commercial buildings for energy efficiency, and most importantly a significantly improved population of large corporate tenants who are proud to be located in such an iconic and sustainable building.

The difference between *engagement* and *transformation and renewal* is that, while there is a direct link between sustainability and business strategy in *engagement,* sustainability *is* the business strategy in *transformation and renewal.*

In the case of Gamesa, wind energy became the core business of the company as it combined its expertise in mechanical systems with its knowledge of aeronautical engineering and materials.

In the case of the Empire State Building, energy efficiency had become a necessary condition for consideration by top tenants, and only by bringing the 70-year old building up to and beyond current standards could it compete in today's market for commercial real estate.

Conclusion

Having looked at six ways that companies have responded to environmental issues over the last 60 years and discussed some concrete examples, the two issues that stand out are the role of corporate governance and the question of ethical conduct.

Governance

In the case of DDT and large chemical companies, the success of using pesticides to fight malaria and improve crop yields might have contributed to the difficulty that people in industry and in government had in considering that these compounds could cause long-term harm to the ecosystem or people. Many members of senior management were also chemical engineers who had experienced firsthand the advancements that chemical technology had brought to the world in the 1940s and 1950s and, for them, the precautionary principle was simply not science. For these people *denial* was the natural reaction.

In the case of the Donora tragedy, the deep belief in the importance of the steel business to the American economy may have made it difficult for senior management, largely long-term employees of U.S. Steel or its bankers, to openly take responsibility for the deaths in Donora. The economic importance of fluoride most likely brought enormous pressure to keep things quiet, pay off the affected people, and move on. The use of the term *cover up* for this type of response does not necessarily imply malfeasance or conspiracy but does reflect a culture at the top that either does not want to know about certain things or takes active steps to keep damaging facts from the public.

The section on *crisis management* and the example of Union Carbide underlies the importance of senior management in setting the tone for the organization and also how deeply embedded cultural traits manifest themselves in a crisis.

At BP, John Browne reported to a board of directors on which Peter Sutherland, an Irish politician and business leader sat as director and eventually as non-executive chairman. Browne's combination of very profitable growth combined with environmental rhetoric seemed to enjoy the full support of BP's board and Sutherland is quoted as saying that BP became a "kinder, gentler oil company." Clearly a firm could not engage in such an ambitious program of *environmental PR* without the support of the board.

The two examples of *engagement* are even more connected to leadership from the top. Toyota's efforts were fully supported by two sons of the founder of the company, Soichiro and Tatsuro Toyoda, who served as presidents of the company up to and after 1992. Likewise, in the case of Henkel the board is dominated by members of the Henkel family whose support of an environmental agenda has been unwavering.

In the two examples of *transformation and renewal* it was Gamesa's initial public offering (IPO) that led directly to its focus on wind energy, because that was the attraction for the investors who bought into the IPO. In a similar way, it was new owners at the Empire State Building who realized that it was time for a fundamental rethink of the building's approach to sustainability.

Right and wrong

As discussed at the start of this chapter, the introduction of six modes of response does not imply a scale of worst to best or even pretend to add an ethical or moralistic aspect to the debate.

The purpose of *Strategy and Sustainability* is to build a bridge between business strategy and the world of environmental sustainability and moral characterizations simply get in the way of making progress. If one accepts the viewpoint of business people discussed in Chapter 1, and the idea that many people were caught off guard, then the six modes of response can be understood.

If one's starting point is that what you and your colleagues are doing is important and righteous, then it stands to reason that the first reaction to the idea that it might cause harm to the environment or people is to not believe such assertions and perhaps enter into *denial*.

When looking at environmental issues that might play out over long periods of time and cause ecological harm, business people may focus more on the short-term financial implications of the firms they manage and down play such issues.

If accidents happen, and there is always a statistical possibility that they will, then there might be powerful forces at play to minimize the public exposure of such events and keep them quiet.

Business people will naturally focus on the cost-benefit side to a specific issue and then introduce statistical probability to measure risk. They will have little to no understanding of environmentalists who say that some risks should not be run and no amount of economic benefit is worth a specific danger such as an oil spill off the coast of a tourist destination.

In terms of its interaction with government, it is also understandable that business people will attempt to work with government to set the rules so that they are favorable for their interests. The definition of those interests is to make money for the company's shareholders in harmony with society but necessarily with nature.

As stated in Chapter 1, these assumptions and values have, in the past, driven the response of business to the environment. Chapter 3 lays out the strategic issues at play so that a new set of alternatives can be looked at and evaluated as business wrestles with how to deal with such issues in the future.

Strategic Issues

It has now become common for firms in developed economies to routinely publish a sustainability report, take steps to increase their energy efficiency, and market some part of their products or services to customers who are in some way interested in their environmental performance. In terms of the modes of responses introduced in Chapter 2, it is more common today to find firms responding with *environmental PR* or *engagement* rather than *denial* and *cover up*.

That being said, there does appear to be a general lack of engagement on the issue of the environment from CEOs and members of the board of directors of the companies in which they serve, and in most cases environmental sustainability has been delegated to the appropriate area:

- Sustainability reports are typically prepared by the corporate communications department, who in turn engage auditors or specialized firms to determine a firm's carbon footprint and other relevant statistics.
- Operations managers are tasked with reducing energy and water consumption for cost reasons and it is up to marketing to work out if branding products or services as "green" makes sense and for R&D to come up with formulations that can be branded in this way.

- Corporate affairs and legal teams are tasked with ensuring that the firm is fully compliant with respect to environmental regulations in the markets in which the company operates.

While such delegation is necessary, there are strategic issues, which senior management may want to be involved with, that might be overlooked or not fully explored if the questions of environmental performance and compliance are simply delegated. The five strategic issues are:

- License to operate.
- Catastrophic risk management.
- Consumer behavior.
- Technological innovation.
- Globalization.

In a 1996 article titled "What is Strategy?"[1] Michael Porter lamented that firms had stopped thinking strategically and were copying each other in a race towards "the productivity frontier" or the best tradeoff between cost and performance available in given industry at the present level of technology and human ingenuity. In his view, real strategic thinking was about making decisions about what to do and not do and finding new ways to compete. Current discussions about value innovation touch a similar theme.

Strategic issues are those that have a material impact on either the medium- and long-term viability of the firm and/or its basic size and scope in terms of geographies and market segments. Strategic issues can be differentiated from operational questions, which, while important, do not pass such a test. Another way of defining strategic issues is by looking at what are included in the responsibilities of the CEO and the board as discussed in Chapter 1.

The five strategic issues just mentioned are derived by looking at what material impacts environmental sustainability can have on a business. The first can affect the very survival of the firm.

License to Operate

In its broadest sense, a *license to operate* indicates civil society's acceptance of a business or a project and a distinction is often drawn between a regulatory license to operate and a social license to operate. While the two concepts are clearly linked there are two important factors that can lead them to be quite different.

The regulatory license to operate is about a company fulfilling its obligation to whatever local, regional, or national governments are involved and having all the necessary permits and requirements needed to operate. If a firm violates the law, in most countries around the world it can be fined, shut down, or even nationalized.

The social license to operate goes beyond that to include the tacit endorsement of civil society; this was first coined by a Canadian Mining Company executive, Jim Cooney[2] in the 1990s and often discussed together with the idea of CSR. Companies that lose their social license to operate can be hit with protests, boycotts, and even violence by disaffected citizens, and such actions can cause tremendous harm to a business in the short, medium, and long term.

The first factor to create a difference between what is legally and socially acceptable is time and, as was seen in Chapter 1, awareness of social issues, such as those dealing with the natural environment, comes in waves. The result of this dynamic is that a firm may be fully compliant with the law at one point in time but still be out of step with civil society, because values can often change faster than legislation and enforcement. Over time, one would expect the political process to incorporate the changing values of the populace into law, thus bringing together the legal and social aspects of the *license to operate.*

A second factor is one of representation and on this issue there are two different aspects to consider. On the one hand, not all governments are fully responsive to the will of the people and thus achieving a legal license to operate in, for example, a military dictatorship, will most likely not have the same legitimacy on the social side as doing so in a parliamentary democracy. This issue will be explored further in Chapter 7.

A second aspect, which will also be picked up under *globalization,* is that often the part of civil society that is most concerned about a specific project or practice might actually live far away from what is happening on the ground and thus attempt to impose their sense of right and wrong regardless of the interests of the local community and their political representatives.

This is certainly the case with many of the environmental interest groups active in different parts of the world today and was also the case back in the 1870s when conservationists from San Francisco urged the federal government to protect the giant sequoia trees in the eastern part of California.

Canadian consultant Ian Thomson structures the process of obtaining a social license to operate coming from legitimacy to credibility to trust, as shown in Figure 3.1.

In building a strong reputation, a firm must first establish its legitimacy by securing all of the relevant permits and legalities as well as opening

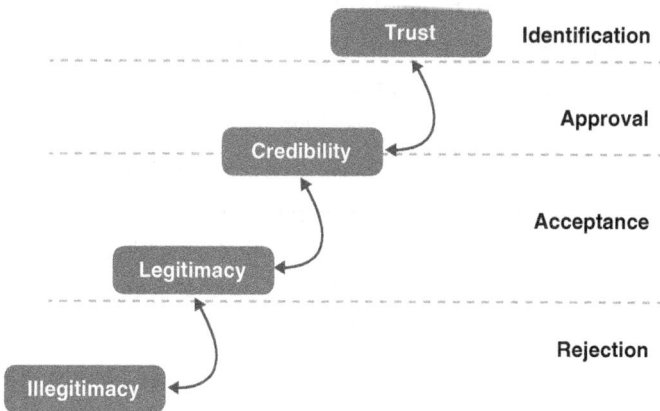

FIGURE 3.1 / Elements of a License to Operate[3]

lines of communication with different stakeholders. This will lead to a firm being at least accepted. For real approval however, credibility is needed, which can only be built over time, and Thompson distinguishes between technical and social credibility. Credibility, in essence has to do with providing reliable information, honoring commitments, and acting in a consistent and responsible manner. For Thompson, the final level, trust, can only happen by creating common or shared experiences between a company and the community around it and this will potentially create a psychological identification with the firm.

What is compelling about Thompson's framework is that it can also be thought of in reverse. A company can put its license to operate in danger if it loses a community's trust and people no longer find it credible. That in turn can put its very legitimacy into question, eventually causing people or interest groups to attack the company using a variety of tactics and tools, which will be discussed in more detail in Chapter 5.

After the catastrophic Deepwater Horizon accident in 2010, for example, BP was in danger of losing the social aspect of its license to operate in the United States. As discussed in Chapter 2, BP had acquired Amoco in 1998 and Arco in 2000 under John Browne's tenure as CEO. Before the accident, the United States was responsible for 26 per cent of BP's production of crude oil, 27 per cent of its gas, and 54 per cent of its refinery output.[4]

Due to a series of public relations gaffs and the ongoing inability to cap the well, BP's CEO lost the confidence of the American public and even President Barak Obama said on television on June 8, 2011 that Hayward "wouldn't be working for me after any of those statements."[5]

In a clear effort to fix the credibility of the company in the United States, BP appointed Bob Dudley, an American who has worked at Amoco for 20 years prior to the merger with BP, to lead the cleanup efforts and a few months later appointed Dudley to group CEO, replacing Hayward.

Another example is the issue of palm oil harvesting, which caught Nestlé by surprise in 2010 when Greenpeace produced a spoof of a Kit Kat advertisement to call attention to the link between palm oil production and endangered orangutans. The video showed a bored office worker taking a break and substituted the candy for a chocolate-covered orangutan's finger, which then covered the workers face and hands with blood as he ate it.

The palm oil controversy centered on a specific supplier, Sinar Mars, that Greenpeace felt was endangering the habitat of the orangutans by expanding their palm oil plantations. Nestlé, which was a member of the Roundtable for Sustainable Palm Oil, had still been sourcing palm oil from the company through its contracts with Cargill, the commodities trader.

After trying to keep the video off the web, Nestlé changed its tactics and chose to engage with an organization called Forest Trust, making a commitment to only use certified oil by 2015. The other thing Nestlé did was to establish a digital acceleration team down the hall from the CEO's office at Nestlé headquarters in Vevey, Switzerland, which monitors virtually every social network in the world so that the company can respond immediately to any threats to its reputation before they get out of hand or go viral.

What is critical about the idea of a license to operate is that while monitoring a company's image and dealing with different media outlets and groups can be delegated to the relevant departments, such as public affairs, corporate communications, and digital marketing, building a culture that ensures legitimacy and credibility is a task for senior management, because only it has the ability to manage issues that may have a significant impact on the business.

That impact can be felt on the revenue side, as disgruntled interest groups can tarnish a firm's reputation or even lead boycotts against a firm or specific products and services. It can also be felt on the cost side, because particular supply sources are challenged and may have to be replaced by higher cost substitutes. Finally, the impact of such events can call into question a firm's survival and be considered *catastrophic risks*.

Catastrophic Risk Management

The key point in the discussion of crisis management in Chapter 2 is that a crisis, by definition, is something out of the ordinary and deals with risks beyond those that are normally discussed, planned for or taken into account in financial projections. One category of risk could be called *catastrophic risks* or risks that have the potential to destroy a company.

In most companies, the role of risk management is to ensure that the company has the requisite collection of insurance policies and balance the cost of that insurance with the risk of exposure to different events. Large-scale, catastrophic risks are often considered out of scope because they are typically not covered by insurance premiums.

In banking, the idea of *catastrophic risk* is well understood as a loss of confidence that can make a "run on the bank." If many depositors choose to withdraw all their money at once, most banks will fail unless propped up by the government. Banks can also fail due to overextension, as happened to Barings, founded in 1762, which collapsed in 1995 after suffering a $1.3 billion loss due to trades made by an employee in its Singapore branch. In 2008 two other iconic investment banks, Lehman Brothers and Bear Stearns, found themselves overexposed to asset backed securities and forced into bankruptcy.

Accepting that the primary role of senior management is to ensure the viability of a company over the medium and long term, then, it stands to reason that the CEO and the board should monitor such *catastrophic risks* and if necessary take action to avoid them.

As shown in the example of Union Carbide in Bhopal (see Chapter 2), firms may be running potentially catastrophic risks connected to the environment. Partly as a result of the Bhopal disaster in 1984, Carbide became the target of a hostile takeover attempt in 1986 and ended up divesting many of its businesses including batteries, packaging and products for the home, automotive, and agriculture sectors. In 2001 Dow Chemical acquired what was left of Union Carbide, originally founded in 1917.

One clear example of *catastrophic risk* is that of a major accident at a nuclear power plant. After a devastating tsunami followed an earthquake that hit 9.0 on the Richter scale off the coast of Japan, the Fukushima Daiichi nuclear power plant was knocked out and its emergency power system was washed away. Without power, it was not possible to cool the reactor, which was close to melting down when valiant firefighters flooded the core with seawater. The flooding caused some degree of radiation emissions but avoided the meltdown, which would have been much, much worse.

The impacts of a disaster at a nuclear power plant are in fact so adverse that no electricity utility could ever bear the costs involved in dealing with such a crisis, and thus they are shielded by law from a total disaster in most countries.

Columbia University's Graciela Chichilnisky, a mathematical economist and expert on climate change, argues that classic decision analysis, which is based on expected outcomes and decision trees, simply does not work when dealing with "rare events with major consequences."

One reason that such calculations do not work well is that the probabilities of these types of events are so low that, no matter how grave the consequences, the expected cost will be low enough to ignore. Another reason is that, during a real crisis, people can become afraid. Citing research into brain activity in situations of fear, Chichilnisky makes the connection that people simply stop thinking rationally when frightened and go into binary modes of fight or flight.[6]

Chichilnisky concludes that new axioms are needed to raise awareness of *catastrophic risks* and bring them into sharper consideration. The lesson for senior management is to periodically take inventory of the *catastrophic risks* facing the firm, to at least have a solid understanding of what can potentially cause them to occur, and to explore the underlying probabilities.

One specific approach, which will be discussed in Chapter 8, is to use scenario planning to uncover such catastrophic risks and look at "what if" scenarios. In terms of environmental sustainability such risks could include:

- Specific release of toxic substances with devastating results such as those that occurred in Bhopal.
- Systemic failure of systems and backup systems, as occurred in Fukushima.

- Unexpected chain reactions such as the explosion of several ships in Texas City in 1947.
- Public protest at specific operations or practices with the potential to lead to impairment or the loss of a firm's social license to operate.
- New scientific findings that prove a substance or practice can be harmful to people or their environment, which lead to heavy regulation or outright prohibition.
- Changes to social mores and values, which lead to heavy regulation or outright prohibition.

Consumer Behavior

For economists who study business strategy, a company builds value by creating goods and services that consumers or other firms are willing to pay more for than the cost of producing the product or service. Once value is created, then one can set a price that shares the value between the seller and the buyer. The amount of value the firm actually gets is often referred to the value that it captures.

The amount someone is willing to pay for a specific product or service depends on the usefulness it has for them or what economists call its utility. This idea can include functional issues such as how well it does what it is supposed to do, quality levels, and also a range of intangible and often emotional attributes such as brand, image, and sense of identification with the product or service.

While it has become fashionable for marketing people to introduce sustainability into a wide array of products and services, what has not been demonstrated in any category besides food is a sizable market segment willing to consistently pay more for products and services that are perceived to be more environmentally sustainable.

In the case of the food category, a number of supermarkets led by Whole Foods (see Box 3.1) in the United States, are developing the category of organic and natural foods and some studies show that a growing segment of households are willing to pay more for such products.

BOX 3.1 WHOLE FOODS

The first Whole Foods Market opened in Austin, Texas in 1980 with the merger of two health food stores in a relatively large 2,500 square feet (1,160 square meter) store that sold a combination of organic and natural food as well as vitamins and dietary supplements.

After some difficult years, the company began to grow by opening new stores in Dallas and Houston, and then purchasing another natural foods company in New Orleans in 1988. Over the next 20 years, Whole Foods perfected its model of buying existing natural food stores and chains and also filling out its network by opening new stores directly.

Whole Foods went public in 1992 and currently has a market capitalization of $20 billion.

By 2014, Whole Foods had a total of 399 stores in 43 U. S. states, Canada, and the United Kingdom and 87,000 employees. Of its $ 14.2 billion sales in 2014, 97 per cent were in the United States and operating income was $942 million or 6.6 per cent, which is about two to three percentage points higher than the industry.[7]

For one of the founders and current CEO, John Mackey, the success of Whole Foods is due to its values-based culture, which stresses its commitment to natural and organic foods as well as its customers' health and team members' happiness as well as a "conscious leadership" style that is about self awareness and emotional intelligence.

Other analysts have determined that Whole Foods is successful because it has tapped into a market where a certain segment of consumers are willing to pay significantly more for food, supplements, and cosmetics that they understand are more natural and therefore healthier. A number of studies have found that in the food category, people, or at least a segment of American consumers, will spend a little more on food they feel is more natural, safer, and grown locally.

The question is how big that segment is: According to a 2012 survey commissioned by Whole Foods,[8] 32 per cent of consumers are willing to pay more for foods without artificial ingredients, preservatives, or colorings, and 30 per cent will pay more for meats raised with no antibiotics or added growth hormones.

Other food retailers have endeavored to copy the Whole Foods model or at least introduce sections in their stores dedicated to organic produce. Whole Foods has reacted to this increased competition by stressing its shopping experience and taking steps to reduce prices and lose its image as costing consumers their "Whole Paycheck" when buying food.

For everything else, from cars, to electricity, to fast-moving consumer goods, it does not appear that there is strong evidence that people will pay more despite literally hundreds of academic papers looking at virtually every facet of the question. Nevertheless, literally thousands of products and services are now being marketed as environmentally friendly or sustainable.

This practice, which could be called green marketing, can be seen as an extreme example of what was called *environmental PR* in Chapter 2 or, if it is done in a much more proactive manner, can also be thought of as *engagement*. There are several strategic aspects that should to be looked at in depth in consideration of such a choice, and these aspects are what ought to bring the issue to the attention of senior management.

The first strategic aspect is to explore the difference between perceived environmental sustainability and real, fact-based, sustainability. While it is said that "perception is reality," simply slapping a green label on a product or service may not be good strategy in the medium term, because it may generate accusations of greenwashing, which can lead to attacks on a firm's credibility.

The second aspect is that the mathematics involved in determining how sustainable something really is can be quite intricate and perhaps even inconclusive. Determining the carbon footprint of anything requires complex technical modeling and large numbers of assumptions, creating space for debate and even deliberate confusion of the issues.

Electric cars, for example, are perceived as "ecological," but whether they are environmentally better than conventional cars depends on where the power comes from, how they are driven, how they are made, and with what materials (see Box 6.2 in Chapter 6).

To do the analysis properly, a life cycle approach should be taken, which looks at the inputs to create, use, and dispose of a product or service, and few consumers or even purchasing executives have the time or even the training needed to go through the calculations to see what is actually true. Increasingly firms are coming to the conclusion that they must undertake such studies despite the considerable costs involved.

The final consideration in this issue is how transparent a firm should be about the life cycle impact of its products and services as full disclosure can be delicate and restricting such findings could open the firm up to charges of covering up its true environmental impact.

The third strategic aspect linked to green marketing is that much of human activity has a negative effect on the environment regardless of the exact formulation, packaging, or power source. Thus any claims of environmental benefit are often about a particular firm's product or service doing less net harm to the environment than another that satisfies the same or similar need. For example, a laundry soap without phosphates causes less water pollution than those with them but is still not beneficial to the environment.

The way this sometimes plays out is that a company makes costly and sincere efforts to reduce the environmental footprint of its products or services, but is still attacked by interest groups and accused of greenwashing due to the fundamental nature of its activities.

Returning to the example of BP from Chapter 2, the company's innovative internal carbon trading scheme did reduce carbon emissions for BP around the world, but Greenpeace awarded John Browne an award for "Best Impression of an Environmentalist" in 1999 because it felt strongly that the carbon footprints of BP's products were what was important, not that of its refineries and logistics system.

A fourth aspect is that when a firm highlights the particularly sustainable aspect of one part of its product line, questions may be raised about the rest of the line. If, for example, a company markets a refillable packaging solution, which is more sustainable than its traditional packaging, does it create the impression that its traditional product, which might have a long history with consumers, is and has been unsustainable?

One particularly useful framework for thinking through the issue of *consumer behavior* in the context of environmental sustainability is Professor Noriaki Kano's way of looking at attributes of product quality (see Box 3.2). What the research appears to be saying is that, while consumers are not willing to pay more money to be green, there is a segment that also does not want to contribute to pollution or global warming and thus have moved over the last few years from not being very interested in the environment to considering sustainability a threshold or "must be" product attribute.

BOX 3.2 NORIAKI KANO AND CUSTOMER SATISFACTION[9]

Professor Noriaki Kano's way of looking at attributes of product quality is particularly useful in thinking through the issue of consumer behavior in the context of environmental sustainability. For Kano, quality and customer satisfaction go hand in hand but, he suggests, there are different aspects of quality.

In his analysis, Kano distinguished between three types of quality in any product or service. Performance quality has to do with those features that have a direct and linear impact on customer satisfaction and perhaps on willingness to pay. A consumer will pay more money for a car with higher horsepower or for a larger diamond. The idea of such attributes is that better performance gives more satisfaction and can often be translated into a higher price.

Kano discusses another type of quality that he calls "must be." These are factors one could call threshold factors or things that the customer will become very unsatisfied without but to which they probably will not attach any importance providing they are there. Such features are often taken for granted.

The third type of quality Kano labels "excitement" and has to do with attributes that a customer will, most likely, not miss but that could sharply increase their satisfaction if present. Excitement factors often impact latent needs or attributes to a product or service that the customer does not even know they feel are important.

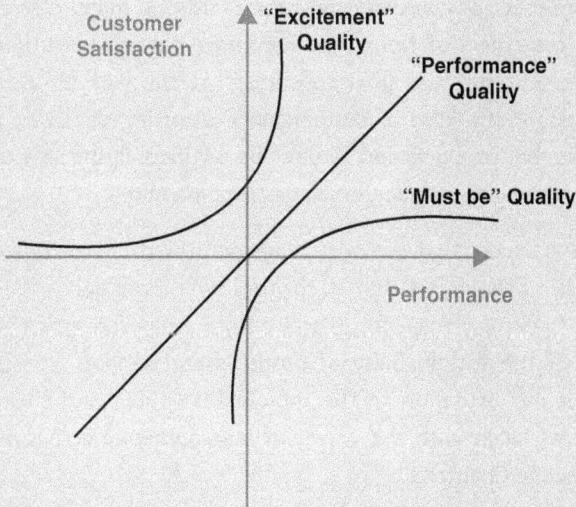

FIGURE 3.2 / Kano Diagram

What typically happens with innovation is that it causes excitement when it first comes out, moves to becoming a performance factor as more and more competitors offer the feature, and then fades away into the background as it becomes a threshold factor or a "must be" attribute.

> *On the issue of environmental performance, there are indi-*
> *cations that for many products and services some minimally*
> *acceptable level is considered a "must be" factor by a significant*
> *number of consumers in markets such as the United States, the*
> *United Kingdom, and Germany.*

If, in fact, sustainability, or some minimum expression of it, has become what Kano would call a "must be" aspect, then engaging in green marketing of one kind or another might prove necessary just to remain in business, despite the issues discussed here.

A fifth aspect of *consumer behavior* is that, in many cases, it is not the actual customers of firms who may have changing attitudes about the environment but the final consumers at the end of the value chain. Increasingly, the kind of sustainability reporting discussed in Chapter 2 requires that products and services be certified all the way up the supply chain, putting the burden on all participants of it.

The final aspect that senior management ought to consider in terms of *consumer behavior* is that it changes over time and what people care about tomorrow may be different from what concerns them today. In terms of the sustainability of products and services, consumers largely did not pay attention to the topic in the 1960s and their interest has risen and fallen with the waves of environmental activism and concern discussed in Chapter 1.

Technological Innovation

The advancement of technology of all kinds over the last 60 years has been remarkable and, in many fields, such as telecommunications, biotechnology, information technology, metallurgy, aerospace, and others, the pace of change has been steadily accelerating promising even more wonders in the years to come.

Managing a firm's technological base is a strategic issue and many companies have chosen to appoint a chief technology officer in order to oversee all aspects of their technological activities; although other organizations may have a chief scientist or vice president of R&D who fulfills a similar role.

Technology is particularly strategic for those companies that are primarily concerned with creating value by developing and distributing complex technological artifacts such as cars, planes, computers, software systems, and a large number of other technologically complex products and services upon which we increasingly depend.

In these and other less technological industries, there are a number of linkages between technological innovation and the environment at the strategic level for which the attention of senior management is recommended regardless of the capability of the science and engineering people in the organization.

The first linkage is the power of new technology to fundamentally alter the competitive landscape of an industry through the introduction of what Harvard's Brower and Christensen referred to as disruptive innovation.[10] Innovation is considered disruptive when the leaders of a given industry do not, for a number of reasons, embrace a new technology when it first comes out. If that technology becomes the new technological standard, those companies may find themselves pushed aside by newer players that have embraced the innovation and can provide products or services that satisfy a different definition of value.

Typically disruptive innovations are cheaper, smaller, or lighter than the technology that has proceeded them and, while they are inferior on some classically important performance attribute, they are good enough for many applications and thus facilitate a change in the order of importance. The typical mechanism for disruption is that such technologies are initially deployed in niche markets and then expand their reach as their technical performance improves.

The link to environmental sustainability is that there are a number of technologies available that do offer a substantially lower environmental impact than conventional solutions but do so at a tradeoff against performance attributes that are considered critically important.

One example of a potentially disruptive technology is electric cars. Today they are more expensive than comparable conventional vehicles, have significantly less range, higher weight, and less internal space for passengers and luggage. For someone who drives themselves to work in heavy traffic every day, they are however good enough and have the added benefit of a certain environmental prestige.

Tesla Motors' all-electric Model S, for example, appeals to a segment of the population who have the money to pay for a luxury sedan and are attracted by its environmental credentials and the ability to charge the cars at home, the office, and at designated charging sites that Tesla is deploying. Tesla sold 20,000 of the cars in 2013 in the United States, which gives it a market share of less than 0.1 per cent and is still very much a niche product.

An example that has proved disruptive is the very rapid replacement of incandescent light bulbs with compact fluorescent lamps (CFL) or low energy bulbs over the last few years. While CFL technology has been around since the 1980s, it was only relatively new societal concerns about climate change combined with less expensive production that kicked off the market.

The bulbs are still much more expensive, have a time delay when turning on, and provide a colder light than conventional bulbs but they were able to disrupt the industry due to their superior energy efficiency and long life. The likely next step is for CFL bulbs to be replaced with the much more versatile LED lighting, which uses even less energy, provides warmer light, and has no time delay. Tracking such environmentally friendly technologies and monitoring their performance is therefore recommended and could prove critically important.

The second link between strategy and environmental sustainability that senior management should consider staying on top of is the potential of new technology to change consumers' and regulators' acceptance of products and services. As technology improves, more information is available concerning the effects of different activities on people and the natural environment and thus, what is considered safe and benign today, can be considered dangerous tomorrow.

In 1957, for example, James Lovelock, developed the electron capture detector, which was able to monitor CFCs and other pollutants in the air, paving the way for the wave of environmental interest and regulation in the 1960s and 1970s. This example demonstrates how the introduction of new monitoring or detection capabilities can provide interest groups with information that can fuel opposition to a firm's activities, and thus it is advisable that the deployment of such technology does not come as a surprise.

The mechanism for covering both issues is to scan the development of technologies that lie beyond the boundaries of the firm and have to do with the larger ecosystem in which a firm's products and services are used. The issue is that there are many advanced technologies available and insufficient time to study them all, especially for senior executives who are subject to extreme time pressure and already have enough on their plate.

The problem with both issues is that unless driven to do so by senior management, technology managers and the heads of business units will underfund the development of potentially disruptive technologies and wide-based technology scanning because of other priorities and limited resources.

Such activities need direct support of senior management either through organization models such as a central research function, earmarked funding, or vigorous and visible political support.

Globalization

As discussed already in this chapter, one of the biggest issues facing many companies is how to manage operations in different regions and countries around the world. Regardless of whether a firm operates in two, ten, or 50 countries and territories, once it leaves its home market, the strategic issues discussed earlier take on additional dimensions. While some of the regional specific ones will be discussed in Chapter 6, the following will highlight how globalization links with each of the other four issues.

In terms of the *license to operate*, international expansion raises potential problems and opportunities both in terms of its legal and social aspects. On the legal side, the regulatory framework is different around the world although there are efforts underway to standardize legal frameworks across trade blocs such as NAFTA, the European Union, and other such arrangements in Asia, Latin America, and Africa.

Legal systems themselves can be different depending on the origin of the country and past colonial ties; and legal compliance in countries such as the United States and the United Kingdom, which are based on common law, means something very different than it does, for example, in most of Europe where legislation is based on Roman law.

In terms of the social *license to operate*, the power of civil society and its ability to influence business and public policy also differs from country to country. In the United States, for example, most people would say there is a balance between society, business, and government and that the press and the courts play a role in keeping that balance.

While some might say that the situation is far from perfect, there are parts of the world where the ruling party or even individual leaders exercise almost total control of the press and the courts, and actually own many of the leading businesses outright. Navigating the differences and nuances from place to place can be challenging to say the least.

To further complicate matters, civil society is now more connected than ever before and thus what a company does in one part of the world can quickly become visible in another. There are a number of examples, such as Nestlé's choice of its supplier for palm oil, discussed earlier, where business practices in one place can affect a firm's perceived legitimacy someplace else.

In fact, what it might take for a company to be successful in one location may affect its social license to operate in another. A very real example faced by many international companies in emerging markets are local competitors who operate at significantly lower levels of environmental protection and cost than they can following their own corporate policies.

The issue even goes beyond the question of legal compliance as an international organization may find itself obliged to apply stricter standards than local law requires in order to avoid causing damage to its reputation in its home market. These stricter standards might impact the firm's competitiveness in the local market. If local suppliers go further than that and actually break the law, due to extralegal arrangements with the authorities, then it becomes even more difficult for the international company to compete.

The fact is that, in many parts of the world, environmental legislation is more lax than in the developed economies because, as will be developed in Chapter 6, there appears to be some correlation between economic prosperity and environmental protection at the city, regional, and national levels as well as the enforcement of that legislation.

Of course, even in the developed economies, standards vary from place to place and political influence can be bought and sold with jobs, investment, or even cash. The problem is that if a firm does adapt to local conditions and lowers its standards then it opens itself up for attacks from special interest groups who oppose such practices.

Such is the case for groups like the Rain Forest Action Network that, between 2000 and 2004, waged a successful campaign to pressure Citigroup to stop funding large projects in the Amazon despite the fact that the projects were fully legal and supported by the local governments.[11]

The example of Union Carbide and Bhopal illustrates another issue connected with globalization and that is the difficulty of managing *catastrophic risks* in far flung corners of the world. Carbide had difficulty communicating with its people at the site and its efforts to assist victims and their families and to probe the causes of the disaster were met with resistance by the Indian government (see Chapter 2).

Finally, in terms of technology management, there is a huge gap between the pace of deployment of certain technologies in different parts of the world and, in fact, the gap goes in both directions between the richer north and less developed south.

In some cases, technologically advanced solutions such as nuclear power plants require a very sophisticated industrial base to ensure that they are safely managed, and thus may not be appropriate in all parts of the world. Likewise, advanced water management solutions may be inappropriate or too expensive for the approximate one third of the world's population who do not even have access to improved sanitation.

On the other hand, low impact packaging solutions such as using soft plastic refills rather than rigid plastic bottles are common in many parts of the world but not yet accepted by most consumers in the wealthier countries.

For senior management, the lesson is to not only look at the growth prospects of expanding to new markets and developing a winning market strategy, but also to take stock of the environmental issues that might derail the expansion efforts or potentially open the firm up to attack in its current and more critical markets, due to unforeseen issues.

Conclusion

The objective of this chapter has been to highlight the most critical strategic issues through which a firm's responses to its natural environment can affect its business strategy or survival.

Stakeholders, such as people who live near a company's facilities, consumers, or even employees, can essentially rescind a firm's *license to operate* if the perception persists that it is somehow harmful to the environment or the people and animals in it.

At the extreme, environmental factors can cause *catastrophic risks*, which must be managed in a proactive way; therefore it might be helpful to provide senior management with training to change the way they perceive such risks, because it is difficult for most experienced business leaders to get their heads around them based on their experience and business education.

Consumer behavior has to do with the potential of some customer segments to either pay more for perceived environmental performance or perhaps to choose a different alternative if some minimum standard is not met. The strategic issue is that, while it is tempting to adopt an environmentally friendly marketing posture, such a strategy can backfire if it is not backed up with a strong commitment to look carefully at a firm's operations and supply chain.

The two strategic issues connected to *technological innovation* are when environmental factors cause it to become disruptive and when the light of science changes how we think about the safety or toxicity of products or services currently considered safe and benign.

The last strategic issue linking the environment to strategy is *globalization*. Since the law and its enforcement are different in different parts of the world, global companies need to choose between maintaining international standards and adapting to local conditions. To make matters more complex, interest groups, and even governments are very sensitive to differences in a firm's approach around the world. What is even more alarming is that such differences may be real, perceived, or even fabricated and have potential to damage a company's reputation.

The question of how a particular firm ought to deal with these issues depends on the industry it is in, its competitive position, the regions of the world in which it operates, and a number of other factors. Chapters 6 and 7 will explore such differences by looking at five different industries and regions as examples.

Before doing that, and also looking in depth at the role played by environmental interest groups, there do appear to be a number of generic strategies that can be used to classify levels of strategic response and these will be developed in Chapter 4.

4
Strategic Options

While Chapter 2 discussed the modes of response that can be observed by looking at how firms have responded to environmental challenges in the past, Chapter 4 considers the strategic options open to business going forward. At the heart of the options is the degree to which business chooses to comply with legislation or do more than the law requires based on an evaluation of the strategic issues raised in Chapter 3. Six strategic options are explored as follows:

- Take the low road.
- Break the law.
- Wait and see.
- Show and tell.
- Pay for principal.
- Think ahead.

The basic idea of *take the low road* is for a company to do the minimum required to comply with the law and customer expectations and take a reactive stance to changes in legislation, society norms, developments by competitors, and other factors. While there is nothing wrong with *take the low road* it might prove risky over the medium term, because many of the issues connected with a firm's environmental footprint may evolve over time and it is possible to be caught off guard, as happened to a number of firms in the past.

Five of the options, including *take the low road*, have full legal compliance as their starting point. The option of deliberately choosing not to comply with some legal aspects is called *break the law* and is explored not to recommend or endorse the option in any way but to examine the risks involved in terms of a potential loss of the legal and social license to operate.

Wait and see not only complies with a company's legal situation today but also takes a more proactive stance and involves preparing the firm to act if and when legislation changes, consumer behavior evolves, or some other factor triggers a change in the strategy.

Show and tell takes its name from a common classroom exercise for small children in the United States in which kids are asked to bring something from home and explain it to their class. The idea behind *show and tell* is that many companies are actually making quite a lot of progress on environmental issues, although perhaps are not fully publicizing all of their activities. In practice, the difference between *show and tell* and *environmental PR*, discussed in Chapter 3, is one of intent. *Show and tell* is about thinking through the choice to transparently tell the company's story, while *environmental PR* has more to do with not making difficult decisions.

Pay for principal, the fifth option explored, is when the board of a company makes a clear tradeoff between certain financial metrics and going beyond compliance due to the ethical viewpoint of key shareholders.

The final option explored is called *think ahead* and is about going beyond what is required today, due to a conviction on the part of senior management that the world is changing in specific ways and that in order to build competitive advantage, hedge against future legislation, or deal with other strategic issues it is better to act sooner rather than later.

Sensibility and Compliance

Every company is in a unique situation in terms of the business it is in, the markets it serves, and the makeup of its shareholders, board, and management team. With this in mind, the following section offers a framework for understanding each firm's starting point with respect to the issue of environmental sustainability. As discussed in the conclusion to Chapter 3, strategic options for the future must be considered in the context of a firm's current position, and thus the applicability of the strategic options introduced earlier for a specific firm depends largely on where it is today.

Figure 4.1 shows the overall framework, which plots *environmental sensibility*, as will be defined in this section, with different degrees of *compliance*, which will also be discussed. The essential idea is that there are potentially robust, strategic options, which will make the most sense for a specific company depending on its levels of *environmental sensibility* and *compliance*.

With a strategic option in mind, then a detailed approach can be developed depending on the specific situation of the company, its industry, and region or regions it operates in.

Environmental sensibility, the vertical axis of Figure 4.1, has to do with the relationship that the people involved with the organization have with

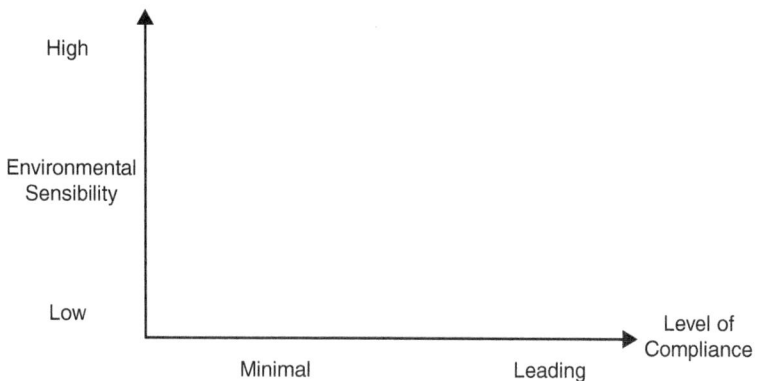

FIGURE 4.1 / **Compliance and Sensibility**

the natural environment. The idea of *environmental sensibility* is, to some extent, linked to the idea of *engagement*, discussed in Chapter 2, with the difference being that *engagement* was presented as a steady state while *environmental sensibility* is considered as a variable idea that can be higher or lower.

Understanding is also related to involvement, which can be motivated by a proactive interest in the environment by some group of people within the firm but also from a reactive requirement to deal with environmental issues due to outside pressure.

A number of factors add up to produce deferent levels of *environmental sensibility* and the purpose here is not to say that more or less is better or worse, but to provide a factual check list to determine what it is. These factors include:

- The nature of the business itself and its regulatory burden.
- The level of commitment from shareholders on issues connected with the environment.
- Outside pressure from interest groups, customers, consumers, and other stakeholders.
- Internal interest on the part of key segments of the firm's employees and managers.

The first factor to consider is the nature of the business itself. Clearly a firm in the business of preparing environmental impact statements will be more involved than one in a business that has little if anything to do with the natural environment such as a chain of hair salons or movie theaters. One could argue that all firms affect and are affected by the natural environment and, while this is certainly true, the environmental impact of movie theaters is significantly less than strip mines or power plants, even if they are located in a place with a warm climate such as Miami and use huge amounts of power for air conditioning.

Another factor that can have an enormous impact on the level of *environmental sensibility* has to do with the level of commitment from shareholders, such as with the example of Henkel in Chapter 1. Another example is Richard Branson's Virgin Group, which is often held up as a model on issues connected with the environment. In those companies where pressure comes directly from shareholders, the firm's senior management will focus on environmental issues potentially even trading off financial returns for ecological value added.

Outside pressure can also serve to heighten *environmental sensibility* either for good or ill as the attention of special interests and the news media will, at the very least, force managers and employees to have an opinion about what the environmental impact of the company is, regardless of whether they agree with the claims by the interest groups.

Finally, there is growing evidence of certain segments of the population at large, and therefore employees, having some level of concern for the environment and a company that strives to be "the employer of choice" may find itself with a degree of internal pressure.

In the case of Union Carbide, discussed in Chapter 2, the perception of Carbide's worldwide employees was one of the critical constituencies that the company struggled to reassure as a result of the tragedy at Bhopal; and many firms find that younger people in affluent countries are increasingly concerned with the environmental footprint of their employer.

The horizontal axis in Figure 4.1 has to do with the level of legal compliance that a company chooses to have with respect to the myriad rules and regulations that affect its operations. While the option of non-compliance is not seriously considered, a firm can take a minimalist approach and simply set out to fulfill all of the legal requirements in each territory within which it operates. Such a situation is perfectly legal and may represent the lowest cost.

Another tactic that many firms have deployed is to apply the rules and regulations of their home market to all countries and territories in which they operate in order to protect themselves against charges of ecological dumping or worse. Other companies take the approach that they must take a leadership position on issues connected with the environment and systematically do more than the law requires.

Harvard's Forest Reinhard calls this going *Beyond Compliance*[1] and argues cogently that good reasons to do so have to do with competitive strategy, increasing differentiation, cost reduction, redefining markets, or hedging against risks in case the regulatory or market environment changes in the future.

Another reason to go beyond compliance could be to attempt to mollify public opinion, and thus forestall the development of more stringent environmental regulations.[2] Industry associations often play a role in establishing voluntary guidelines and then lobbyists work to persuade regulators that there is no need for further regulations.

Figure 4.2 adds the six strategic options discussed already to the framework mentioned earlier in order to illustrate, in general terms, which strategy might make the most sense depending on the level of *environmental sensibility* and *compliance* in which a specific company presently finds itself.

As can be seen in Figure 4.2, the six strategic options array themselves along the diagonal axis of sensibility and compliance. Thus a firm that currently has a minimal level of compliance and very low sensibility probably has little choice but to *take the low road*, at least for the time being. *Wait and see* implies slightly higher levels of both compliance and

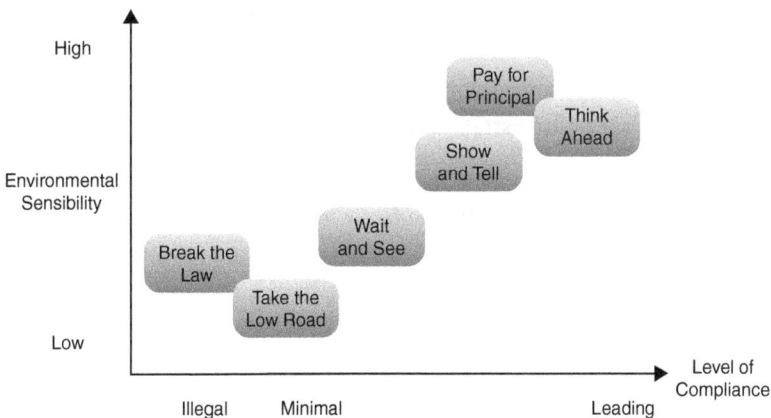

FIGURE 4.2 / **Strategic Options**

sensibility, and even more sensibility is required to fully implement *show and tell*. Both *think ahead* and *pay for principal* are about adopting leading positions in terms of compliance but perhaps different levels of sensibility.

Interestingly enough choosing to *break the law* actually requires a higher level of environmental sensibility than simply complying with it, because some level of risk analysis and cost–benefit ought to have been executed before pursuing such a choice.

As stated emphatically here, with the exception of *break the law*, there is nothing inherently right or wrong about adopting any one of the five options discussed and what makes sense for one firm will be very different from what makes sense for another.

While the scales for both sensibility and compliance shown in Figure 4.2 are only illustrative, each of the six strategic options are explored in sequence, as the capabilities or functions that need to be developed are essentially cumulative in nature. Thus a firm can move from one option to another by adding additional capabilities.

Take the Low Road

The first strategic option shown in Figure 4.2 is referred to as *take the low road* and depending on a company's circumstances it may be the most rational approach. The basic idea is to minimize the cost of compliance due to the understanding of the CEO and the board that environmental issues are of little strategic importance to the firm.

While many ecologists would say that all firms (and people) have a significant environmental impact, the fact is that some have a much greater impact than others. In many retail businesses, for example, the key issues are to get prime locations in strip malls and shopping centers, train employees, and keep the cost of goods sold as low as possible and sales high by appealing to the mass market.

The owner of a food franchise with just over 100 outlets, for example, has adopted a positioning based on what sells in the food court, that is, taste, value, and fun. In this case, none of the senior management team, the franchise owners, the employees, or the customers have any specific identification with environmental issues and the approach is to comply with state health and safety laws, dispose of the used cooking oil in a responsible way, and leave it at that. This chain, for example, chooses not to have outlets in California due to the increased regulations of doing business in the state.

Energy and climate control is often provided by the shopping center in any case and specific stores have little say in decisions about the energy mix, level of air conditioning, and lighting. If the chain were, however, one of the nation's largest, then the situation would be very different, as was the case with McDonalds and the issue of packaging. In November 1990, faced with an increasing number of cities banning styrofoam and under pressure from its customers, McDonalds worked with the Environmental Defense Fund and abandoned its traditional "clamshell" box for hamburgers and replaced it with paper and cardboard. The new packaging had 90 per cent less bulk and represented total cost savings for the company but, according to McDonalds' officials at the time, the driver to change was public perception and pressure.

In terms of the framework shown in Figure 4.1, the difference between McDonalds and the much smaller chain of restaurants mentioned in the earlier example is its public profile, which increases its environmental sensibility.

In a business with low environmental impact and with little or no legislation affecting it, the environmental sensibility of senior management, employees, and even customers may, in fact, be quite low making a *low road* approach a realistic option. From a strategic point of view however, what is important is to make the choice explicit and work through the strategic implications.

In the first place it is important to be sure that neither the legal nor social license to operate can be placed at risk due to environmental issues and that there are essentially no catastrophic risks on the horizon. To do this, some sort of periodic risk assessment is advisable and can be effectively outsourced to specialist firms.

Once the analysis is done, operating units can be instructed as to what level of compliance is required and an effective reporting and control system can be put in place consistent with the risk analysis.

The second issue to check is customer attitudes and behavior with respect to environmental issues and again this can be done mainly with external market research, although at least some minimal sensibility should be developed within the marketing function.

Another assumption that lies at the heart of the *low road* approach is that there is no disruptive technology on the horizon that can alter the fundamental competitive dynamics and/or customer behavior with respect to environmental issues. Again, a periodic review of developing technologies could be a sound idea and, depending on the depth of the company's R&D function, this could be done by the firm's own engineers or outsourced.

The last thing to do is to check that the basic assumptions about regulations, competitors, and customers apply across all of the regions and countries in which the company operates including its extended supply chain. As discussed in Chapter 3, Nestlé was taken by surprise by Greenpeace's campaign against its purchase of palm oil even though Unilever had been singled out for the same issue the year before.

In terms of organizational responsibilities, it will be important for a member of the senior management team to drive the periodic reviews mentioned to make sure they get adequate budget and that their findings are taken into account. If the firm already has an environment, health, and safety (EHS) unit, this group should be adequate to the task, although it may be necessary to supplement it with specialized consultants. If there is no such unit then its creation should be considered even for a firm pursuing the *low road*.

Depending on the company, EHS is normally located in corporate services, R&D, or human resources (HR). For a small firm, such as the one in the example mentioned earlier, such an analysis can be done via outsourcing or perhaps, in a limited way, by one of the owners simply spending some time reading up on such issues.

Outsourcing major periodic reviews makes sense for a *low road* strategy as the entire objective is to keep costs low and not build internal capabilities if they will later not be used. Fortunately both auditing and strategy firms have developed practice areas in sustainability that are well equipped for this type of task and there are a number of individual advisors and consultants available for smaller firms.

If a firm does choose the *low road* approach, what is very important is to make that choice explicit and carefully communicate it to the unit managers around the company. The delicate aspect to the communication is that managers could easily misinterpret a *low road* approach for implicit permission to cut corners and take risks with respect to compliance.

Thus, even in this option, it is necessary to not only instruct local units to understand legal requirements and follow them but also to build a monitoring and control system in order to ensure that the firm is fully compliant with the law in all of its operations around the world.

What most characterizes the *low road* as a strategic option is its reactive nature. Perhaps what sets it apart from the de facto strategy of firms that have been caught off guard by environmental issues in the past is the idea to periodically look at the situation and make an informed decision not to do more than is required. A decision to deliberately do less than what is legally required actually involves a slightly higher degree of sensibility and is referred to as *break the law*.

Break the Law

While this strategy can not be recommended, there is a temptation for firms to do less than the law demands when the cost of compliance is high and there is the perception that there is little downside to non-compliance. The perception that the downside is low can be a combination of there being little or no economic penalties associated with discovery, a low probability of that discovery, or both.

As will be discussed in Chapter 6, there are many parts of the world where the degree of environmental regulation has gotten far ahead of the public administration's ability to enforce the law, and thus the temptation for malfeasance, that is, deliberately taking shortcuts or ignoring regulations, becomes very real. In other parts of the world there are myriad rules and regulations and these sometimes even contradict each other creating "wiggle room" for those companies intent on finding ways to lower costs.

The strategy of *break the law* should not be confused with that of a firm that opts for *taking the low road* and unwittingly goes over the line. In this case, senior management will take steps to correct a problem as soon as it is detected. In *break the law*, senior management must make an effort to either deliberately avoid specific rules or regulations or set up internal processes so that such infractions occur at a statistically incredulous frequency.

While the legal risks associated with *break the law* are decidedly out of the scope of this book, the fact is that governments increasingly are attempting to prosecute deliberate or even unintentional damage to the environment in the criminal courts. This is particularly true when human life has been lost as a result of environmental calamities, such as the case of Union Carbide in Bhopal discussed at length in Chapter 2.

What is clear is that there are strategic risks to pursuing *break the law* that may, in fact, outweigh any legal issues associated with the strategy. These have to do with the possibility of being found out, not by the government, but by motivated interest groups who might jump on the issue of non-compliance to attack the company and put its legal and social license to operate at risk.

The last issue associated with *break the law*, which touches on a deeper issue, is that if senior management either directs its employees to disregard rules and regulations or sets up a managerial system in which they are encouraged to do so, then it is requiring its own people to behave in an unethical manner. While this might seem more or less important, the question is that if a manager is encouraged or allowed to infringe on certain rules, then what is to stop him or her from also breaking others?

Perhaps an oversimplified example is that if the company asks an individual to illegally dispose of certain types of waste or to pay off environmental inspectors, how can the firm stop them from cheating on their expense account or take kickbacks themselves?

As already mentioned, a final aspect of *break the law*, which is shown graphically in Figure 4.2, is that it actually requires a higher environmental sensibility than simply taking the *low road*. This idea, which may appear counterintuitive, is that to deliberately avoid compliance, one must first calculate the cost of that compliance and then perform some sort of cost–benefit analysis to determine that it is better to not comply. In contrast, a company pursuing the *low road* need not actually know its cost of compliance as a separate line item in its profit and loss accounts.

Wait and See

Moving up the diagonal of Figure 4.2, the next strategic option is to do a bit more than the minimum in terms of compliance but to take a much more proactive stance in terms of monitoring environmental issues in all five of the strategic issues discussed in Chapter 3.

The strategic logic of *wait and see*, is to be ready to adjust the firm's practices, offering of products and services, and communications policies if and when it is determined that it makes sense to do so. At least four functions are key to making *wait and see* work.

The first key function is to develop a process for knowing what the legal requirements are for technical issues associated with each operating unit and to track their compliance with hard data. Building such a process is not a trivial task as very often such data is not currently built into the central reporting systems and it is critical that such an effort be comprehensive and cover all the jurisdictions in which a firm operates. Depending on the business these may be local, regional, and national and the volume of data can become overwhelming fairly quickly.

The data required may also not be currently available even at the operating unit level or, alternatively, be delegated down to a managerial level where managers speak only their local language and are unaccustomed to centralized reporting, thus creating a serious management challenge just to find out what is going on.

The second key function required for *wait and see* is to also understand and track the firm's portfolio of products and services in terms of their environmental footprint both in production and in their usage, again in order to know what the current status is.

Similarly to the case of technical data, the footprint of products and services may not currently be included in a central place, or even be available, so that putting together even a snapshot might be a daunting challenge.

With these two elements in place, the third key function is to actively monitor trends in legislation, consumer response, and the activities of environmental interest groups and social media in order to be able to spot emerging trends. The challenge on this issue is that responsibility for looking at what is happening is normally spread out across different units such as operations, supply chain, marketing, and public affairs.

The last key function is to prepare different levels of management in advance for the possibility that the company may need to react at some time in the future. While this effort may not require the same level of dedicated time and energy as building the other capabilities, changing a firm's managerial culture is a complicated process and can take years to accomplish. If a firm, for example, has traditionally only measured its managers on financial performance, it will be almost impossible for them to suddenly embrace a new set of environmental goals at some future point in time, if some groundwork has not been done in advance.

As discussed, it makes sense to outsource periodic reviews of the company's situation in the *low road* option. In *wait and see* there is an implicit acceptance that environmental issues will increase in importance over time, and thus it makes more sense to develop internal capabilities and to make the process of knowing the firm's current situation continuous and build such knowledge into its management systems.

Thus when a firm chooses to adopt *wait and see*, environmental sensibility will increase as a result of following the strategy and that increase is, in fact, a pre-requisite for the strategy's success.

The result of collecting the technical data will be to begin to raise the awareness of environmental issues amongst those responsible for operations and management control. The same will happen when marketing teams are asked for the environmental footprint of their products and services and legal and corporate affairs executives are asked to track environmental legislation and interest groups.

In terms of the men and women managing the firm, it will be important to involve them in the effort to understand the company's current situation and make the choice of *wait and see* explicit. Bringing line managers into the process will naturally increase their environmental sensibility.

From a capabilities point of view it may be that the current EHS organization is sufficient for the task, but it may also be the case that a slightly different or broader skill set is necessary including, for example, change management skills. Lately, it has become fashionable to create a position with the title of sustainability director or even to simply rename EHS as sustainability and add the firm's activities on CSR to the mix.

The key in implementing *wait and see* is to give the task sufficient visibility to be sure that data concerning the current situation is actually found and that all departments contribute. What many firms have found to be very successful is to set up a cross functional group of senior managers to lead the effort, calling it the "sustainability council" or some similar name.

The advantage of this approach is that it not only serves to sensitize managers about the issue and prepare them for eventual action, should the need arise, but also makes sure that all functions and business units are involved and provide their piece of the puzzle.

Such a council can be managed by a technical manager but should be led by a member of the senior management team in order to ensure that all units take the effort seriously, show up for scheduled meetings, and provide the requisite data.

What is also important for a firm that is following *wait and see* is to take great care with its communications to the outside world, because the main objective of the strategy is to minimize the cost of compliance and avoid taking action until it can be shown to be in the medium- and long-term interest of the firm. While this basic idea can be compelling for business leaders, it might be perceived as cynical by outside interests, and even regulators, and can open the company up for criticism if not managed well.

Taking a proactive communications stance requires a higher level of environmental sensibility than is normally found in a company following *wait and see* and also a level of compliance that is more than legally required in specific areas. That strategy is referred to as *show and tell*.

Show and Tell

Chapter 2 discusses a mode of response referred to as *environmental PR* and the strategic option of *show and tell* is about choosing to go beyond public relations (PR) by increasing the *environmental sensibility* of senior management, line managers, and even hourly employees.

In management seminars with second and third level managers of international companies, it is striking how little they often know about their own performance in the area of environmental sustainability. Such companies normally publish annual sustainability reports and may have dedicated teams working on the issue, but what distinguishes *show and tell* is the incorporation of a firm's environmental performance in its internal and external communications such that it becomes part of the culture and brand identity.

In terms of compliance, choosing *show and tell* requires applying relatively high standards in all countries and territories in which it does business, because the higher the public profile, the more scrutiny will be directed by interests groups and regulators. Often the most logical choice is to adopt the environmental standards they have in their home market as their own internal code of conduct.

The strategic rationale for choosing a *show and tell* strategy will most likely come from a conviction that the firm's customers, employees, or perhaps other critical stakeholders value, to some degree, its commitment to the principals of environmental sustainability.

Customers may in fact be willing to pay more for the company's goods and services or at least consider it a necessary condition to continue to do business. A high profile may also be required to attract and retain employees, as discussed in Chapter 3, or to please a government minister or elected official who values the firm's commitment, due to conviction or even cynical electioneering.

The danger with *show and tell* is that, if serious problems are uncovered or even unfounded accusations are made, the entire effort can be written off as greenwashing by activists and potential damage can be done to the firm's reputation. Evidence of a double standard between developed and developing countries can be used by activists to challenge the social license to operate and a catastrophic incident such as Bhopal or Deepwater Horizon can open the firm up to tremendous criticism.

Thus the most important capability for a firm pursuing a *show and tell* strategy is to have very well developed internal processes to assure accurate and real time data concerning its environmental performance in every market it operates in and the internal controls and culture in place to ensure that corners are never cut and compliance is assured.

The second capability is to have a strong communications team who can get the word out but also have the technical skill to appreciate the very complex mathematics involved in measuring energy and water consumption, parts per million of contaminants, a firm's carbon footprint, and many other such details.

The third critical capability is to have robust financial models in place such that the cost of compliance and going beyond compliance in certain areas is well known and can be rationally considered by senior management. As mentioned earlier, modeling a firm's environmental footprint can become quite complex and translating that impact into economic risk and reward requires special skills and the trust of senior management.

The fourth key capability is for senior management itself to be fully fluent in the concepts to do with environmental sustainability such that it can not only consider issues and choices at the highest level but also communicate them easily and in a compelling way to the press, shareholders, community groups, and government representatives.

The final and most difficult challenge in deploying *show and tell* is to begin the process of encouraging virtually every part of the firm to look for areas where its environmental footprint can be reduced, to make progress, and to communicate that progress both internally and externally.

In terms of organization, in some cases a firm will take the step of appointing an executive to lead its efforts in sustainability; this person can be more or less senior in the hierarchy and report into different people including the CEO. One solution is to explicitly recognize the importance of communications and put the sustainability manager in corporate communications alongside the managers of shareholder communications and internal communications. Part of the rationale for this approach is that a firm following *show and tell* will certainly be publishing a regular sustainability report and messaging should be consistent between it and the financial information published on a regular basis.

In any case it is important that whoever is responsible for the area has access to the senior management team in order to assure that information travels freely up and down the organization and that they can assist directly with developing speeches and presentations.

Typically a small team is also useful to help get the word out across the company, develop and deploy training programs, and provide other functions. Monitoring and control can be set up as independent units but also can be built into the internal audit function, which normally resides in finance or even in a compliance office.

Finally, a firm pursuing *show and tell* will need a technical group that can do the necessary technical analysis to understand the environmental impact of the firm's operations and products and services, and again this can be separated out or embedded in the firm's R&D function.

Compared to *taking the low road* and *wait and see*, choosing *show and tell* will add significant costs to the business. The main source of added costs will be to develop functional capabilities that will, most likely, require some number of dedicated people. For a relatively small company perhaps only a small team would be needed, but such initiatives tend to grow by themselves once started so it is critical that the CEO and the board make the decision to go ahead with *show and tell* with a full understanding of its costs.

The costs must then be contrasted with a clear understanding of the benefits of taking this option. The strategy, if executed well, should have a positive impact on the firm's environmental image, which may increase sales or margins, depending on consumer behavior, have a positive impact on the firm's share price, make it easier to attract and retain talent, or perhaps have some other benefit in terms of a reduction in energy costs or an improvement in community or government relations.

If the business case for *show and tell* is not forthcoming, then its adoption should be considered very carefully, because once a firm begins to proactively and systematically share its environmental performance it will be very difficult, if not impossible, to stop at some later date from a PR and regulatory point of view.

When the business case is not compelling and some group of shareholders feels it is important to go down the path of *show and tell*, or even go further, the strategic option is referred to as *pay for principal*.

Pay for Principal

As a result of the waves of environmental interest discussed in Chapter 1, a number of entrepreneurs, venture capitalists, and public officials found themselves in agreement with environmental activists who had largely been out of the mainstream in the past.

This group includes high profile people such as Richard Branson mentioned earlier, John Doerr of Kleiner Perkins, Patagonia's Yvon Chouinard, and Al Gore who besides being a politician has also gone into business and sits on the board of significant companies such as Google. There are, of course, significant numbers of people with a lower profile who also have deep conviction about the environment and choose to bring these values into the companies they work for, invest in, or set up.

Due to their convictions, many of these people actively encourage the companies they are involved with to take a proactive and leading role in taking steps to either minimize their environmental impact or offset whatever impact they do have with other activities. When such a person has a controlling interest in the company or is able to drive its strategic agenda, then that company may go beyond what is required by law and go further than *show and tell*.

In this case, the fundamental rationale is not a medium-term business case but a deep belief that reducing air and water pollution, protecting the natural landscape, or taking active steps to mitigate climate change are critically important tasks and should be part of the corporate agenda. Some so called B corporations have this focus.

Writing in the *New York Times Magazine* in 1970, Milton Friedman rallied against what he called corporate philanthropy and equated it with theft.

Friedman's point was that if a company is going to give money to charity, or any cause, it must get the money from someplace. It may pay lower dividends to shareholders, charge its customers higher prices, or reduce the wages and benefits of its employees. His view was that it would be better to let shareholders, customers, and employees choose what to do with their own money and not make that decision for them.

For many business leaders, doing more for the environment without a compelling business case amounts to more or less the same thing and

Friedman's critique could be leveled against *pay for principal*. What sets it apart from corporate philanthropy is when the direction to adopt such a strategy comes directly from shareholders who have a controlling interest in the firm.

In this case, Friedman's charge no longer applies as it is these shareholders who choose to sacrifice some part of their dividends, or take some market risk, with their own money.

What is critical is that the strategy is explicit so that other shareholders can freely choose to be a part of the effort, and make the same choice, or sell their holdings. What confuses the issue is that the entrepreneurs involved in such projects often hold out a different rationale for their choices and put forth their own ideas about how business and environmental sustainability can be done hand in hand without tradeoffs or cost–benefit analysis.

In some cases, what has happened is that the company has actually latched on to a market segment that identifies with environmental sustainability and gives their business to the firm because of its positioning or perhaps is even willing to pay higher prices. In other cases the firm's position gives it a very strong social license to operate or attracts talented employees, again giving it some clear and compelling competitive advantage.

In other words there may be a compelling business case based on the strategic issues discussed in Chapter 3 that perhaps has not been systematically articulated, which explains the positioning. To be fair to brilliant entrepreneurs such as Whole Foods' John Mackey, who wrote a book called *Conscious Capitalism*,[3] the initial motivation to shape such companies may have been based on principal rather than deep analysis or market research. Thus when such people become extremely successful, it is completely natural for them to articulate that success in terms of their commitment to principal rather than business strategy.

A company pursuing *pay for principal* will have many of the processes discussed in *show and tell* in place but will most likely do even more on some particular aspect of environmental sustainability, such as offering a line of carbon neutral or naturally produced products alongside its more mainstream brands, products, or services.

The challenging part of managing in such an organization is to distinguish which aspects of the business strategy make sense in clear strategic terms, such as attracting the customer base for Patagonia or Whole Foods, and which attributes may not be so clear.

For a manager responsible for a particular aspect of the business that is a pet project of the CEO or leading member of the board, it may be politically difficult to show unfavorable numbers concerning profit and loss and return on investment (ROI).

Investing in the most efficient aircraft and flying slightly slower flight plans, can, for example, reduce the carbon footprint of air travel. Richard Branson's company, Virgin Atlantic, is committed to reducing its carbon emissions per passenger mile by 30 per cent between 2007 and 2020, among other measures, and the question is to what extent is this policy driven by the opportunity to reduce fuel prices, a perception at Virgin that its customers value the company's commitment in this area, or the passion that Branson brings to the issue?

Like many of the issues connected with environmental sustainability, answering such questions requires sound technical data, deep consumer insight, and complex mathematical models to tease out the different aspects of the question.

What is key therefore for pursuing *pay for principal* is clarity of thinking on the part of the CEO and periodic revision by the board of the assumptions upon which the strategy is based, explicitly separating those aspects of it that already make sense in terms of clear business criteria and those that are a function of conviction and principal.

Communication with the public, shareholders, and regulators will be even more critical in *pay for principal* as sustainability is a central part of the firm's positioning and message.

Going back to the example of Virgin, a slightly different formulation of the question could be: What type of fleet will the price of jet fuel, regulators, and the traveling public require of an airline in 2020? Changing a fleet of airplanes takes time and what might be at work is a conviction, on the part of Branson and his colleagues, that the successful airline of the future will be much more efficient and have a lower carbon footprint, in terms of tons of CO_2 per passenger mile than the industry average today, and that the best way to secure the future is to act now.

That strategy, that is, doing things today to prepare for a future in which environmental concerns are thought to be more prevalent, is referred to as *think ahead*.

Think Ahead

As discussed in Chapter 1, the last 60 years have seen increasing environmental interest and regulations and this has occurred in waves often provoked by some specific incident or the cumulative impact of a number of factors.

As each wave triggers the interest of the general public, politicians try to respond to or capitalize on that interest and enact legislation in response. Legislation often mandates increased regulations and the setting up of institutions to monitor and control those regulations. Perhaps the most important aspect of this pattern from a business standpoint is that such mechanisms and bureaucracies do not go away after the wave of interest has passed but entrench themselves in society and become the "new normal."

Thus each wave builds on the level of the environmental sensibility of the general public and regulators in a cumulative fashion, such that doing business in many countries requires much more environmental awareness and compliance than it did 25 or 50 years ago. As will be discussed in Chapter 6, environmental concern and regulation also seems to move from more mature economies to developing countries.

What these two trends seem to indicate is that it is likely that the level of concern and regulation in the future will be higher than it is at present, which could lead the senior management of a company to consider the strategic option of *think ahead*.

The argument for *think ahead* is that if society's attitudes about certain industrial practices do shift and require a more environmentally friendly approach, they may do so quite quickly and business leaders could be caught off guard as they have been in the past. The question then becomes: Can a firm react quickly enough to respond to changing circumstances or is it necessary to begin such development years in advance on the chance that such a shift might come to pass?

From a risk management point of view, the issue is to avoid putting a firm's legal or social license to operate in doubt if its current practices fall afoul of changing norms. A simple example is when production plants are initially located far away from urban centers but find themselves 20 years later surrounded by new residential neighborhoods. Levels of noise, pollution, and heavy truck traffic perhaps were acceptable in the countryside but might not be for suburban residents sometime in the future.

In terms of market positioning, it takes years to develop a trusted positioning and if society is suddenly willing to pay more for a perceived environmental benefit or unwilling to work with companies that do not have some minimal baseline, then it is possible to miss a lucrative opportunity or, worse, lose business to a competitor that is perceived to perform in a more sustainable manner.

With this idea in mind, one of the key functions needed for *think ahead* is an ability to reflect on trends and imagine the future. For this purpose forecasting, as a discipline, is insufficient and a firm will need to develop its capabilities in the area of scenario planning, which involves developing clear constructs around multiple possible futures and is explored further in Chapter 8.

Another key function that is also required is a very well developed change management process, such that it is possible to predict how long it will take to increase the firm's environmental sensibility and compliance level in the case it decides to do so.

If, for example, it is thought that five years is required to change the culture such that it can support a *show and tell* strategy, then the firm should embark on implementing such a culture at least five years before it is required by competitive and market dynamics.

Fixed assets such as fleets of ships and airplanes, manufacturing plants, pipelines, and mines require many years to develop and need to be productive for many years in order to generate positive returns. Changing the structure of such assets requires time and thus, in some industries, it might turn out to be strategically critical to adopt *think ahead*.

While the development of scenarios and the technical work involved can be delegated to specialists, only senior management has the ability to drive such an effort. As a pioneer of scenario planning, Pierre Wack, argued that the key lesson of going through such a process is not the scenarios themselves but the learning that the senior management team accrues by going through it.[4]

Another issue that requires the direct input of senior management is that predicting the future is a tricky business, and it might take more time than thought for a specific issue to come into the consciousness of the general public or regulators. Thus a firm might spend a great deal of money and energy preparing for a future that is then delayed or perhaps does not occur.

In this case, competitors who did not make the investments will have a competitive cost advantage against one who did. This example highlights the importance of senior management being deeply involved in the process so that it can take full responsibility whatever the result.

Thus an additional key function for successfully implanting *think ahead* is to accurately track the assumptions about the future on which the strategy is based, and to develop the strategic flexibility to speed up or delay initiatives based on the evolution of those assumptions. The challenge is that this effort will most likely cross functional lines and can involve people from finance, marketing, corporate affairs, operations, and R&D.

The stakes can be quite high for a *think ahead* strategy depending on the size of the investments made relative to the size and financial strength of the company. On the downside is the risk, mentioned earlier, of doing too much too soon and finding the company having higher investment levels or higher operating cost relative to competitors who did not make the investments or change their processes.

On the other hand, is the possibility of sudden shifts in the way the general public, consumers, regulators, and other interested parties, such as investors and financial institutions, see specific issues and the time it may take a firm to react. The management team of an airline, for example, might choose to buy more efficient aircraft much later than Virgin or not at all. The problem might come at some point in the future if the flying public chooses only those airlines with a minimum carbon footprint and Virgin is perceived to have a compelling competitive advantage.

Conclusion

As shown in Figure 4.2, there are a number of strategic options that a firm can choose depending on its level of environmental sensibility and compliance and, in the absence of some moral conviction, there can be no "right" answer to this question – although, for obvious reasons, *break the law* is not recommended.

In a businesses with low environmental impact and little environmental sensibility on the part of customers, employees, shareholders, and other stakeholders one might find it relatively simple to comply with regulation and *take the low road* could be the most reasonable strategy.

The four other legal choices offered represent increasing the level of both compliance and the environmental sensibility of the organization. As detailed in this chapter, there may be compelling business reasons for a firm to do more than the law requires, including reducing costs and appealing to customers, employees, or other interest groups.

The choice of pursuing *wait and see* or *show and tell* should be taken based on a clear understanding of the costs and benefits involved in today's marketplace and regulatory environment. In the absence of such a compelling argument, a firm's leadership may choose to go beyond compliance for two possible reasons. One is that individuals with a controlling interest in the company believe it is the right way to go because of their own ethical or moral convictions, and this is the idea behind *pay for principal*. The second is that senior management and the board have been convinced that the future will require a different level of engagement and that the firm should *think ahead* and act now in order to be prepared and/or avoid costly remedial action and potential liabilities.

One aspect of the future environmental scrutiny under which firms will be placed is the behavior of environmental activists and thus Chapter 5 will explore these groups in detail in order to better equip managers in understanding who they may be facing today and what kind of organizations they are likely to face tomorrow.

5

chapter

Environmental Interest Groups

From a strategic point of view, it is essential that business leaders understand the environmental interest groups that are often the first organizations to raise awareness on specific issues and attempt to mobilize the press, public opinion, and eventually regulators. An important point is that not all groups with an environmental agenda are the same and some are easier to engage with than others.

While there are literally tens of thousands of such groups, some are better organized and funded than others and may have millions of members, significant assets, and a large number of full time staff. Others may be no more than an individual with a Facebook account and deep conviction. Part of the challenge in dealing with these groups is to distinguish which is which, although in today's hyper connected world a video can "go viral" in a matter of days, regardless of how large or well established is the organization or individuals who produce and post it.

What does seem to be useful is to distinguish between four broad types of organizations and then explore issues of reputation, membership, and funding within each category. The first group of organizations, which represent the beginnings of environmentalism, will be referred to as *conservationist* organizations. Such organizations represent all parts of the political and ideological spectrum but can be considered collectively because they generally share, as their primary objective, the goal to protect the beauty and richness of large tracts of nature even while much of the rest of the planet is made over for human use.

The second type of organizations that are discussed in this chapter tend to be more radical in their approach than the *conservationists* and differ from them in terms of focus, tactics, and objectives. These organizations are referred to as *activists* and are often concerned with one part of the natural world such as oceans, rain forests, and the arctic or perhaps one particular practice or technology such as nuclear power, forestry, genetic modification of crops, and so on.

While the focus of *conservationists* is normally tied to specific places, *activists* see themselves as defending every place and typically engage in much more direct, and even illegal, activities to make their point.

The third group of organizations are associations of neighbors or citizens concerned with a very local problem or perceived problem having to do with a specific project or place. Such groups will be called *localists* due to their primary focus. While *localist* groups have been active even before environmental issues first came into the public conscience in the 1950s and 1960s, they have begun to wield significantly more influence in the last few years thanks to their ability to amplify their message using the internet and social media.

The final category of organizations explored are referred to as *advocates* and, while they are difficult to categorize by topical or philosophical viewpoint, what they do have in common is a genuine willingness to reach agreements between business, civil society, and government for what they perceive to be the common good. While some of these organizations are not for profit, others operate as service companies, lobbyists, or consultants.

Over the last ten years or so, there has been an increasing polarization of opinion concerning the environment and environmental protection and that has led to a blurring of the lines between these different types of groups, making it more difficult for business to know how to engage and respond to them.

Specifically, *conservationist* groups have been becoming increasingly *activist*, involving themselves with local issues. At the same time, *localist* groups are progressively reaching out to form alliances with each other, making them behave more like international *activists*.

If this sounds a bit confusing, the reality is that it is often difficult for business leaders to understand who they are dealing with and, without a clear idea of who is on the other side, it is almost impossible to make progress. This confusion, in fact, is what has given rise to the *advocates*.

Before going into the nature of each one of these groups, the Sierra Club will be discussed in depth as, over time, it has been an excellent example of all four types of organizations. As in other sections of the book, many of the examples provided, such as the Sierra Club, have a strong focus in the United States and Canada, although some examples from other countries are also mentioned.

The Sierra Club

What would later become the heart of Yosemite National Park was first protected by the federal government in the United States in 1864, despite local opposition. One of the truly magnificent redwood trees had been cut down by lumbermen and its trunk was shown around the world as a tourist attraction. Public reaction to the felling of the trees led to the act that protected one of the oldest groves. In the 1870s, conservation writer John Muir led a group of San Francisco naturalists to lobby the government to expand Yosemite and make it the Nation's second national park after Yellowstone in Wyoming.

This group called itself the Sierra Club and elected Muir as its first president. In terms of the classification described earlier, the Sierra Club, at that time, most resembled the kind of grass roots, *localist* organizations that we see today. Throughout the late 1800s and into the next century the focus of The Sierra Club was on protecting specific parts of the wilderness in the western United States, including the Grand Canyon and Mount

Rainier, and organizing hiking trips, or outings as the club calls them, for its members.

In 1910, the organization fought and lost the battle to dam the Hetch Hetchy river near Yosemite in order to supply water to San Francisco about 180 miles away. At issue was the lack of a secure water supply for the city and, in this case, the politics were too compelling for even Muir's friend Teddy Roosevelt to stop. The dams were built and today the system provides water to 2.4 million people in the San Francisco Bay area.

The fight over the Hetch Hetchy was an example of the Sierra Club working to protect a specific place from development that would characterize much of its activity until the early 1960s. A supporter of the Hetch Hetchy project was Gifford Pinchot, the head of the U.S. Forest Service, who was also close to President Roosevelt and felt that the best way to protect the country's forests was to manage them and balance conservation with the needs of the surrounding communities, including the lumber industry. The issue created a breach between the club and the Forest Service, which has endured to the present day.

In 1916, the United States created a different organization, the National Park Service, to manage protected areas and tapped Stephen Mather, a Sierra Club member, as its first director. In 1927 the State of California made its own state parks commission and made Sierra Club secretary, William Colby, its first chairman.

A degree of tension between the Sierra Club, the Forest Service, and the National Park Service would characterize the club's development for the next 50 years, during which it continued to organize outings for its members and work to expand the state and national park systems and protect them from encroachment by dams and industrial development with a clearly *conservationist* agenda.

The club worked for the establishment of the Alaska's Admiralty Island, Joshua Tree National Monument, and Dinosaur National Monument, as well as Point Reyes in California and Padre Island in Texas. While the geographic scope of the club's activities gradually spread from California to other parts of the United States, its primary focus was to set aside or conserve parts of the country as nature preserves and pointedly not to be involved in what happened outside of the parks.

This approach gradually began to change when, in 1952, the club appointed its first executive director, David Brower. Up until then the club had been run on a day-to-day basis by volunteers and its 15-member board. Brower, an avid mountaineer, became first involved with the organization by participating in a series of expeditions it had arranged and under his leadership the club began to expand its activities in several directions.

In the first place, Brower began to aggressively open new chapters in the Pacific Northwest, Nevada, the Great Lakes, Texas, and other places. Brower is also credited with popularizing the club and increasing its membership by selling a series of very attractive books with vivid photographs of wilderness and nature, some of which featured photographs taken by Ansel Adams.

By the late 1960s, however, Brower had taken a more *activist* stance on many issues and a schism emerged within the Sierra Club between him and more traditionalist members of the board. Brower spent more time in New York working on books and full page ads in east coast papers, taking an increasingly strident tone on a range of issues including nuclear power, water pollution, and others.

Brower's *activist* stance and publishing activities led the U.S. Internal Revenue Service to cancel the club's tax exempt status in 1966 and while this increased the financial problems of the club it also resulted in an increase in membership as a result of the positive publicity that the club received. All in all, the Sierra Club's membership grew almost tenfold under Brower's leadership going from 8,000 members in 1954 to 75,000 in 1969.

When the club's finances began to deteriorate the situation became untenable and eventually, when a group of more traditional minded people were elected to the board, Brower resigned. Brower went on to create a more *activist* organization, Friends of the Earth, and Michael McCloskey became the new executive director after serving initially in an acting capacity.

McCloskey was a lawyer who had initially thought to go into politics but lost his first election and joined the Sierra Club as an organizer in the Pacific Northwest. There he developed a highly legal and political approach to pushing back against the U.S. Forest Service, lumber companies, and other developers successfully protecting millions of acres of wilderness and building out the local Sierra Club chapter organization. After that he headed the club's national efforts on conservation before succeeding Brower.

McCloskey's tenure at the Sierra Club coincided with the tremendous burst of environmental awareness at the end of the 1960s and the Earth Day celebration discussed in Chapter 1. Reflecting back on those times, McCloskey refers to how he and the club president, Phil Berry, chose to deal with the wave of environmental activity:

> In the face of changing times and new competition, Phil Berry and I both decided that the Sierra Club should position itself as a strong player. We would take on all of the new issues, use all of the latest tools, and attract as much support as we could. We would work actively to flesh out our organization throughout the country. We would assume a high profile and take risks. In this new time, we would seek to become the best-known and most productive environmental group working on public policy.[1]

During McCloskey's tenure the club organized a legal defense fund and started to get involved in political lobbying and filing suits on behalf of a number of issues and causes, including halting the development of supersonic aircraft; supporting The Native Claims Act in Alaska; banning DDT; and supporting the Clean Air Act, the Ports and Waterways Act, and the National Forest Management Act. In many ways McCloskey took the club down the same activist path that Brower had begun to pursue, but did so in a more behind the scenes way and by working through the political process.

The Legal Defense Fund of the Sierra Club can be compared to other *advocate* organizations, which will be discussed further, and has continued to the present day alongside the club's ongoing activities in support of a number of parks and national monuments. Specific issues the club has become involved in include continued opposition to nuclear power, opposition to the confirmation of U.S. Interior Secretary James Watts in 1981, publicly condemning the Exxon Valdez accident, and most recently promoting solar power and renewable energy.

While essentially focused on the United States, the Sierra Club joined other groups to protest the World Bank's support for Indonesia's logging of its rain forests, and teamed up with Amnesty International to obtain the release of Russian environmental activist, Alexander Niktin.

After McCloskey, the club proceeded along three parallel paths. One was to follow its *conservationist* history working at the local, regional, and national level to organize, litigate, and lobby. A second set of activities was about organizing outings and trips and continuing to build its membership. The third was to take an increasingly *activist* stance on key environmental issues.

By 2010, the transformation of the Sierra Club into a much more *activist* organization could be considered complete with the appointment of Michael Brune as executive director. Brune had started his career as an organizer for Greenpeace and had led the Rainforest Action Network for seven years, during which time the organization ran a number of successful campaigns including changing Home Depot's lumber purchasing policies.

In 2013 Brune and 47 other Sierra Club *activists* were arrested in the first example of civil disobedience in the organization's 120-year history. The action was in protest of the Keystone XL pipeline, which would permit Canada's export of the oil produced in the Alberta Tar Sands, and – while the issue is complex – the change in style and approach by the club is an example of how far it has moved from its roots.

The Sierra Club illustrates all four types of organizations that business finds itself dealing with on environmental issues. The club was founded to protect a specific place, Yosemite, and in its first years was active on a number of very specific projects in California such as the Hetch Hetchy River. This focus gradually shifted to one of promoting the national park and monument system as a way of setting land aside and conserving it. In the 1960s and 1970s the club shifted again and first built its own advocacy group before becoming much more *activist* on a number of fronts.

Today it is a large organization with 2.4 million members in 64 chapters, a $40 million budget and a staff of 500 people. While continuing to work on conservation, it is increasingly *activist* on specific issues yet still organizes 20,000 outings per year for its members.

Conservationists

As discussed in Chapter 1, the conservation movement has its roots in the 19th century and found inspiration in the writings of Ralph Waldo Emerson, Henry David Thoreau, and many others.

Conservationists come from all parts of the political and ideological spectrum and are brought together by their desire to assure that we protect the beauty and richness of nature in specific places. While there are literally thousands of such organizations around the world, some of the oldest and most well funded are shown in Table 5.1, which still includes the Sierra Club despite the much more *activist* stance of its executive director.

Roger Scruton, the philosopher cited in Chapter 1, associates conservation with conservative politics, because its purpose is to leave things as they are. He cites examples of hunting and fishing associations in the United Kingdom leading the way to preserve and protect the natural environment and points out that hunters, in many places, have replaced natural predators such as wolves and mountain lions in keeping populations of deer and other animals within sustainable limits.

The relationship between business and conservationist organizations has been generally positive over time, although there have been specific

TABLE 5.1   Partial List of *Conservationist* Organizations

Organization	Year Founded	2013 Budget (USD)
American Forests	1875	5,000,000
The Sierra Club	1892	N.A.
The Wildlife Conservatory	1895	230,000,000
National Audubon Society	1905	87,000,000
The National Wildlife Foundation	1936	85,000,000
Ducks Unlimited	1937	163,000,000
The Nature Conservatory	1946	717,000,000
Defenders of Wildlife	1947	31,000,000
Trout Unlimited	1959	41,000,000
World Wildlife Fund	1961	266,000,000
African Wildlife Foundation	1961	23,000,000
The National Wild Turkey Foundation	1973	53,000,000
Pheasants Forever	1982	63,000,000
American Birds Conservatory	1994	11,000,000

instances of tension. Part of the reason for the positive relationship is that many senior managers and board members also have a deep love of nature and are largely supportive of the goals of such organizations. In many cases, the boards of directors of the conservationist organizations also have a number of business people on them who add modern management experience as well as fund raising capabilities.

Friction between *conservationists* and business usually happens when the logic of industrial expansion or suburban sprawl impacts directly on a specific natural reserve or regional issue in which the organization is deeply involved. In many cases regional or national associations come into conflict with local business interests and this, as discussed in Chapter 1, was the origin of the National Parks System in the United States and other countries.

For business, dealing with *conservationists* is conceptually straightforward as the basic logic is one of tradeoff. A negotiation might result in an agreement to protect a wilderness area in exchange for opening up other land for development. A group might be convinced to publicly support a mining project, for example, as long as the project is confined to a certain territory and that the company commits financial support for other projects that the group is interested in.

Part of the tension between Brower and the board of the Sierra Club back in the 1960s resulted from a compromise worked out in California between the Sierra Club president, William Siri, and Pacific Gas and Electric to locate a nuclear power plant in Diablo Canyon rather than the environmentally sensitive Nipomo Dunes area.

This kind of process is exemplary of what is required when dealing with *conservationists* and the utility eventually decided that the cost of resiting the plant was considered reasonable to achieve the Sierra Club's support. Brower, according to McCloskey, had come to take a position against any and all nuclear power and attempted to withdraw the club's support. He had become an *activist*.

In terms of the strategic issues discussed at length in Chapter 3, engagement with conservationist organizations can be part of an effort to protect, improve, or establish the social and even legal license to operate, for example in the nuclear power plant mentioned earlier. By securing the blessings of the Sierra Club or a similar organization, companies can rightfully claim to be protecting the interest of the natural environment for public and official constituencies.

Endorsements from *conservationist* groups can also have an impact on consumer behavior, or at least potentially shape the perception of an organization if done as part of a broader strategy of environmental engagement. The danger of trying to use such endorsements too directly, however, is that, if the firm's commitment is not deep or broad enough, it can open itself up to attacks from more *activist* groups who will endeavor to point out any internal contradictions of a company's actions in order to bring public pressure to bear.

Activists

While the roots of the conservationists lie in the late 19th century, environmental activism was born in the peace movement of the late 1960s and early 1970s. The first and foremost of the *activist* organizations is Greenpeace, which was originally formed to stop nuclear testing in the Aleutian islands in 1971.

The origins of Greenpeace are well documented as many of the protagonists went on to write books about their experiences and, while the different accounts highlight personal and political differences, what is clear is that the primary motive was to try and disrupt the American government's atomic testing program on Amchitka island.

The American Navy intercepted the Greenpeace ship long before it reached the testing site and the test did go forward as planned. What happened next, however, was that the attempt gained wide publicity and became what Greenpeace would later call a "mind bomb," causing so much media attention that the U.S. government eventually decided to suspend the testing program in Alaska.

While the small band of Greenpeace *activists* who first challenged the U.S. Navy did so without much hope of success and very little deep strategy,[2] today, activists are fully aware of how to use every tactic and technique to further their particular agenda.

In one of the founders' accounts, Patrick Moore documents how Greenpeace went from opposing nuclear testing to the commercial fishing of whales and then to the annual baby seal hunt, and how the tactics evolved into a kind of playbook for calling attention to something and then deliberately putting an organization's social license to operate in play in order to force it to change its policies and practices.

Moore would eventually split from Greenpeace as the organization continued to grow in size, complexity, and also in scope eventually targeting many aspects of modern society including fish farming, forestry, and PVC pipe.

Table 5.2 lists some of the oldest and best funded activist organizations and, again, there are many such groups including some, such as the Earth Liberation Front, which are, in fact, underground if still operative at all.

Following the path set by Greenpeace, the primary strategy of activist groups is to threaten a company's social license to operate by calling

TABLE 5.2 **Partial List of *Activist* Organizations**

Organization	Year Founded	2013 Budget (USD)
Environmental Defense Fund	1967	134,000,000
Friends of the Earth	1969	20,000,000 (est.)
Greenpeace	1970	293,000,000
Natural Resources Defense Council	1970	108,000,000
Earth First!	1979	N.A.
Green America	1982	3,000,000
Surfrider Foundation	1984	7,000,000
Heal the Bay	1985	4,000,000
Rain Forest Action Network	1985	4,000,000
350.0rg	2008	5,000,000

attention to practices it sees as damaging to the environment in general or whatever specific issue the activist organization is concerned with. The Kit Kat video mentioned in Chapter 3 is an excellent example of where Greenpeace successfully challenged the essential marketing message of a Kit Kat, which had to do with treating oneself to an indulgence. By linking that indulgence to the killing of orangutans in Indonesia, the idea was that consumers would withdraw their support of Nestlé and buy a different chocolate bar or snack food.

Another example of deliberate attack that could threaten a firm's license to operate was the Rain Forest Action Network's campaign in the 1980s against Citicorp for participating in loans destined for projects in the Amazon. Following the activist playbook, protests were targeted at Citicorp accusing the company of destroying the rain forests. Embarrassed by the exposure, Citicorp developed sustainable lending guidelines that it follows 30 years later.

While tangling with activists over a specific issue is unlikely to threaten the future existence of a company, real damage can be done in the court of public opinion, which can eventually lead to litigation, changes in legislation, and medium-term damage to a firm's public image.

It is in this sense that a company that chooses to embrace a publicly forward stance with respect to its environmental credentials, such as that described in the strategy of *show and tell* discussed in Chapter 4, must take care to assure its performance is consistent across the board. The issue is that, if there are practices somewhere in its global operations or in its supply chain that contradict the public messaging, *activists* will seek out those practices and expose what they might see as hypocritical behavior.

If part of the logic behind taking such a forward stance was to influence consumers' buying decisions, then the strategy could backfire. Perhaps the biggest challenge in dealing with *activists* is that they are not necessarily satisfied with a firm changing its practices or developing new technology in order to mitigate the problem. As the goal of *activists* is often the complete elimination of a practice they perceive to be harmful to the environment, any kind of compromise can be perceived by these "deep environmentalists" as selling out.

The final issue, which makes dealing with *activists* very difficult for managers and business people, is their somewhat ambivalent and even casual use of science. On the one hand *activists* tend to support the application of the precautionary principal discussed in Chapter 1 to its fullest extent and grab at any scientific support for whatever point they are trying to make, even when it is tenuous at best. On the other hand, they will reject scientific arguments that do not support their ideological point of view and in fact demonize any scientist who is on the other side of the debate.

Such attacks can become very personal and destructive creating a kind of scientific censorship that makes it politically incorrect to support certain points of view or question the scientific basis of some ecological campaigns. In these efforts *activists* play on, and in some cases foment, the idea that much of science has been subordinated to the interests of big business. However, while there are a number of well documented cases from the past where this was true, most leading scientific journals and universities have policies and procedures in place to protect the neutrality of scientific thought such as the peer review process.

Localists

As has been mentioned, the third type of group business often has to deal with are associations of neighbors or citizens concerned with a very local problem or perceived problem having to do with a specific project or place. What is of particular relevance in dealing with *localists* is the passion and energy they bring to their cause, because it's normally personal for them and has to do with issues such as the health and safety of themselves and their children, the value of their homes, and the future of their community.

Business leaders may be tempted to write off such groups as being ill informed, because very often the scientific or technical underpinnings of their position might be weak, flawed, or even non-existent. In discussing a food safety issue, for example, one leading executive of a food products company expressed frustration with "mommy bloggers" who had no basis in fact.

While it is certainly true that the scientific underpinnings of *localist* opposition to a project or technology can be unconvincing or even wrong, there have also been instances when they have been proven to be tragically correct.

Such is the case of Love Canal in New York State discussed in Chapter 1. Although the problems at Love Canal were initially exposed by local journalists, it was a concerned mother, Lois Gibbs, who created a *localist* group, The Love Canal Homeowners Association. She and her neighbors eventually managed to get the Environmental Protection Agency and U.S. President Jimmy Carter to support the community, resettle the families involved, and get the site cleaned up.

Business must in any case tread carefully with *localists* because passions run so high and the David versus Goliath story line is always interesting to the news media regardless of the facts of a particular case.

One technology that has received tremendous opposition from such groups in the last few years is wind power. A typical example is the

Australian organization called Stop These Things. The following is taken from the "About Us" page on their web site:

> We are a kitchen table group of citizens concerned about what is happening across rural and regional Australia, by the harm being done by the wind industry, in partnership with governments.[3]

At the time of this writing, the National Wind Watch, a group that opposes wind energy, had identified over 120 groups like Stop These Things in the United States, 62 in Canada, 74 in the United Kingdom, and dozens more around the world.[4] Typically, opposition to wind energy is a very specific, local argument, which essentially argues that large, utility scale wind farms are unsightly and harmful to local inhabitants and wildlife.

In fact, James Lovelock, who developed the Gaia hypothesis and is briefly mentioned in Chapter 3, agrees and is a staunch opponent of wind energy, because he feels it ruins the landscape from a visual perspective. For him, despoiling the country in order to power wasteful cities makes little sense.[5]

In Australia, Stop These Things takes these arguments further, insisting that the science behind wind energy is fraudulent and the entire industry is just a scheme to transfer taxpayers' money to wind energy developers who are, by its definition, corrupt.

Similar groups oppose the lumber industry in specific forests, large scale solar plants in deserts, hydraulic fracking in regions and counties, and countless other examples. What is similar in looking at these groups is that their membership is passionate about the cause for which they are fighting and normally not open to compromise and debate. Such groups are formed to stop a particular project or technology in a particular area and as that is the group's reason for being, like the *activists* mentioned earlier, no compromise can be tolerated.

The only positive end point for *localists* is to win their battle and have the forces of darkness (as they perceive the industry or company involved) go somewhere else. As already mentioned, this is not an acceptable position for *activists* who are concerned with the universal eradication of a practice or technology they perceive as harmful.

This willingness to allow things to go elsewhere has opened up *localist* organizations to charges from other environmental groups that they are really saying "not in my back yard" or simply being referred to as NIMBYs. The criticism is that such groups are not really concerned with the environment per se but only with their personal safety, housing values in their community, or their own desire to maintain the beauty of their surroundings.

Roger Scruton is largely sympathetic to the *localist* viewpoint and uses the term *Oikophilia*, which means love of a particular place, household, or what we consider home. He draws the term from Greek meaning the "love of beauty and respect for the sacred."[6]

Scruton has, in contrast, little time or patience with transnational entities that try to determine what is right and wrong for people in their own communities. For him, sovereignty resides with the local community and thus their sense of what is aesthetic and pleasing is the most important aspect in developing local policy.

The key strategic issue at play with *localists* is the social license to operate in a given place or community. They will protest, launch petitions and legal challenges, and even resort to civil disobedience and potentially sabotage in order to achieve their objectives.

An extreme case is that of Julia (Butterfly) Hill, an activist who spent 738 days living on a platform on a specific redwood tree in Humboldt County, California until an agreement was reached in 1999 with the Pacific Lumber Company to protect the tree.

One of the challenges for business leaders dealing with such opposition is that it defies their own internal logic and common sense. In opposition to building large scale concentrated solar projects in the middle of the Mojave desert, for example, a group called The Wild Lands Conservatory mobilized a U.S. Senator, the Sierra Club, and others to oppose siting projects in part of the desert that is relatively close to Los Angeles. The logic of the group's leader, David Meyers, was the pristine beauty of the desert, corridors set aside for the passage of Big Horn Sheep, and five tortoises who belong to an endangered species.[7]

For a wind farm developer who thinks in terms of kilowatt hours, investment costs, and rates of return, and already believes that the wind industry is a positive force on the planet, such concerns for a piece of practically empty desert are hard to fathom.

A second challenge in dealing with such groups is to accurately understand the level of support they have in a given community and to determine who, in fact, they really are. The internet is, almost by definition, somewhat anonymous and democratic in the sense that a web page can look quite professional when it actually only represents the views of a few individuals. At some point during the political process, there will be public hearings or live demonstrations and sometimes that is the only way to know what kind of support such groups really command.

The final strategic issue in dealing with *localists* is that, using social media and the internet, they can beneficially link up with other, similar groups in other locations. Eventually, if their organizational capabilities are sufficient, they can create wide spread opposition and even begin to behave like the larger, more well-funded *activist* organizations discussed earlier.

Advocates

While classifying environmental groups into the three types discussed in this chapter is useful, there are a number of organizations, consultants, and lobbyists, who do not fit neatly into the categories of *conservationists*, *activists*, or *localists*. Many of these groups and the individuals who lead them have their roots in the environmental movement but have, like Patrick Moore, moved on to something else, which they describe in different ways.

While much is different about such groups, companies, and organizations, they will be referred to as *advocates* because they do seem to share four characteristics.

The first characteristic is that such organizations recognize that improving the natural environment must be done with one eye on human development and that sustainability brings together society, the economy, and the environment. They tend to reject the idea put forward by some *activists* that mankind itself is the problem.

The second characteristic is that such groups do not profess neutrality in the major debates connected to business, society, and the environment, but defend or advocate a specific agenda. What differs widely across the spectrum of organizations is the particular viewpoint or angle that they defend, because the issues connected with this broader definition of sustainability are quite complex and well-meaning *advocates* might find themselves on different sides of a specific issue.

A third characteristic, which is very important for business, is that *advocates* will generally work within the political process to advance their ideas and, in fact, often embrace and even champion plural forms of discourse such as international panels, round tables, conferences, and other formats in order to make progress. In some cases *advocate* organizations will be asked to drive the process of building consensus as they can often bring professionalism to a specific debate. While they might have a specific goal in mind, they will often remain open as to which aspects of a solution or a compromise between different interests ought to prevail.

The fourth characteristic that *advocates* generally share is a respect for the scientific method and an understanding that data, or at least good data, can and should be used in order to have fact-based discussions.

While there are a large number of such groups and organizations, Table 5.3 shows a few big companies that could be considered *advocates*.

The Rocky Mountain Institute (RMI) is an example of an *advocate* organization. Founded in 1980 by Amory and Hunter Lovins in Colorado, RMI has been focused on energy efficiency and creating a low carbon economy since long before the topics became popular. RMI sees its role as a catalyst for change and often brings together different players to discuss solutions to systemic problems. RMI is funded by a combination

TABLE 5.3 Partial List of *Advocate* Organizations

Organization	Year Founded	2013 Budget (USD)
Union of Concerned Scientists	1969	23,000,000
Worldwatch Institute	1974	21,000,000
The International Energy Agency	1980	30,000,000
The Pew Charitable Trusts	1974	300,000,000
The Rocky Mountain Institute	1980	13,000,000
Forest Stewardship Council	1993	20,000,000 (est.)

of philanthropy and limited consulting engagements and also has spun off entire departments when it is thought that they can survive as going concerns.

For business, *advocates* often offer the best opportunity to find a willing partner with whom to engage and they, in turn, might prove helpful in dealing with other groups. Here a slight distinction ought to be drawn between *advocates*, as discussed here, and consulting companies, which are increasingly developing their capabilities in the environmental space.

While some *advocates* will take on consulting engagements, they will only do so if they are in line with the goals of the organization itself. In the words of one director of such an organization, they see their role as providing encouragement and knowledge transfer, and being catalysts for the change they are committed to. Consultants, on the other hand, will provide advice based on their customer's needs and will typically not push their own agenda because they are client, as opposed to, issue focused.

Conclusion

Chapter 5 has described four types of environmental organizations that a specific business may find itself dealing with, and these are summarized in Table 5.4.

Business will find itself dealing with all types of groups, depending on the issues involved, and the involvement of senior management may

TABLE 5.4   Types of Environmental Organizations

	Conservationists	Activists	Localists	Advocates
Focus	Nature	Problems	Projects	Solutions
Scope	Wild places	Every place	Someplace	Problems
Key Strategies	• Lobbying • Legal battles • Engagement	• Confrontation • Media relations	• Confrontation • Social media	• Negotiation • Round tables • Workshops
Funding Model	• Members • Services • Grants • Donors	• Members • Donors	• Campaigns • Donors	• Clients • Donors
People	• Professional • Technical • Sincere	• Volunteer and professional • Political • Passionate	• Ad-hoc • Local • Emotional	• Full time/ part time • Technical • Committed

be essential either in the discussions themselves or in developing the strategy, which can then be deployed by the community relations and corporate affairs teams.

The key idea is to try and understand when one is dealing with technically-oriented professionals who will work towards finding compromises and solutions, or when the people on the other side are committed zealots or frightened neighbors.

Advocates and *conservationists* can largely be relied upon to play by certain rules and allow themselves to be influenced by facts. The key to engaging successfully with these kinds of groups is to be ready for real concessions and have funds available to back up promises. If an organization is not really willing to find compromises, then engagement will only lead to disappointments and possible escalation. If there is a genuine willingness to engage, then win–win solutions can be found.

Committed *activists*, on the other hand, need to be managed in a very different way, because it may be difficult to get any type of agreement with them. Thus there is little sense in arguing about the site selection of a nuclear power plant with a group that is against the technology at all costs. In this type of situation, it may make more sense to isolate such groups by engaging in other parts of the political process such that the local community will support the project or practice.

Finally, *localists* need to be treated very carefully as emotions can run high when peoples' homes and families are involved. In these cases, companies must make an effort to fully understand the *localists'* concerns and also to try and gauge the degree to which a specific group truly represents the will of the community. If the concerns are valid and/or representation is high, then they need to be addressed. If concerns are simply untrue, then education is the only path forward, but again must be handled with care and perhaps through trusted third parties such as *advocates* or *conservationists*.

6

chapter

Industry Examples

There are important differences in the way the five strategic issues that were covered in Chapter 3 play out in different industries. This chapter will thus explore those differences, by looking at five examples, and discuss how each industry's relationship with the environment has developed and look at where it is today. The apparent strategy of specific companies will also be looked at using the strategies introduced in Chapter 4.

The five industries were chosen for their relevance in terms of environmental impact and/or their value in illustrating points raised in the opening paragraph. As a comprehensive treatment of the relationship between any one of these industries and the natural environment would require at least a separate volume, the focus in this chapter is simply to use the examples to illustrate the issues at play.

The oil and gas sector is central to the modern world and is also partially responsible for many of the greenhouse gasses that are produced when its products are consumed. The industry thus is exposed to much attention because of its activity and is also deeply involved in the political debate associated with climate change.

The transportation sector produces 13 per cent of the world's CO_2 emissions and cars, trucks, and busses also produce local air pollution, which, in some cities, is a much more urgent problem.

The fast-moving consumer goods industry is discussed here because of the importance of consumer behavior to the industry as well its vulnerability to attacks by *activist* organizations. Mining is also interesting because the idea of a license to operate was developed initially in this sector, which has also been the target of *activist* and *localist* groups.

The last sectors under discussion are the information technology and consumer electronics businesses, which will be looked at together because of their relationship to each other and their collective potential to reduce global energy consumption through digitalization and combined power requirements and environmental footprint.

Oil and Gas

The oil and gas industry provided 56 per cent of the world's energy needs in 2012[1] and is responsible, in many ways, for the prosperity we currently enjoy. Economic historians trace the rise in world population, income, life expectancy, and health to the access to relative cheap energy over the last 130 years or so. Today the industry moves approximately 34 billion barrels of oil and 3,500 billion cubic meters of gas on an annual basis[2] and is a key component of the global economy.

As they became popular in the late 1800s, kerosene, gasoline, and other petroleum products were considered to be environmentally superior to the alcohol fuels and whale oil they replaced. While the industry did suffer from spills, fires, and waste, the issue of the industry's relationship to the environment did not really emerge until the 1950s and 1960s in parallel with the growing concern about the environment discussed in Chapter 1.

Today, oil and gas companies are constantly under attack by *activist* organizations, particularly when accidents happen. There is also significant opposition by *localist* organizations for specific exploration projects and *conservationists* get involved when leases are offered for exploration in or near protected areas. One issue that unites all types of groups as well as more moderate *advocates* is the development of the industry in the Arctic.

Similar passions are aroused with respect to the relatively new process of hydraulic fracturing or fracking to access tight oil and shale gas. While Greenpeace and other activists have come out against fracking, most of the opposition is coming from localist groups who are concerned about the safety of the water supplies in their communities.

In the United States these interests are in conflict with local landowners who have received windfall profits from the industry and people who work in the gas fields. In Europe and Oceania, the issues are different as the government typically owns mineral rights, meaning that localist groups fight the practice while the national energy ministries typically support it.

Surprisingly, the routine traffic of oil tankers and liquefied natural gas (LNG) does not provoke much opposition except for localist concerns about specific LNG terminals. The issues that are normally raised are oil spills and climate change.

Oil spills

One of the first public expressions of concern about oil spills came from residents living near the Houston Ship Canal who formed a *localist* group in the 1950s to complain about the contamination of the water.[3] In the late 1960s, a series of accidents created momentum to regulate water pollution and to pass legislation restricting the industry's offshore drilling, transportation, and refining operations.

These events included the grounding and spill in 1967 of an oil tanker called the Torrey Canyon in the United Kingdom, a more significant spill caused by the blow out on an offshore platform near Santa Barbara, and an oil fire on the Cuyahoga river in Cleveland, Ohio. Oil spills and discharges would continue through the 1970s and 1980s leading up to the catastrophic spill of the Exxon Valdez in 1989.

The Valdez incident would eventually cost Exxon $3.5 billion[4] in damages and also resulted in the passage of the landmark Oil Pollution Act in the United States, which greatly increased the legal liability of tankers and oil terminals.

Differences in the world's demand for oil and its geographic location have created a tremendously large and complex logistics operation with hundreds of oil and product tankers at sea on a continuous basis. Accidents do occur from time to time, such as the grounding of the Prestige off the coast of Galicia in Spain in 2002.

The Prestige called attention to the fact that, as a result of tighter environmental laws in the United States and other wealthy countries, ships are increasingly registered in countries with less of a legislative burden. The Prestige, for example, was owned by a Greek shipping company but registered in the Bahamas as a Liberian vessel. It had a single hull as opposed to the more expensive and safe double hull design of U.S.-flagged ships built after 1989.

The other major incident, described in Chapter 3, was the blow out and explosion of the Deepwater Horizon drilling rig in 2010, which will likely cost BP more than $10 billion as well as serious damage to its reputation.

The industry's primary response to oil spills has been to continuously improve its drilling and production technology and also to create the Oil Company's International Marine Forum in 1979 in London after the grounding of the Torrey Canyon mentioned earlier. The Forum produces research, runs tanker safety programs, and lobbies on behalf of the industry, stating that its central objective is to promote the safe operation of the maritime operations of the industry.

An example of the work published by the Forum is a paper on the efficacy of the use of double hull tankers. The report concludes that while double hulls do reduce the likelihood of oil spills, they require proper construction and preventive maintenance in order to be effective.[5]

The challenge for ship owners is that, with some exceptions, it is difficult to justify employing the latest technology and most expensive crews on the basis of willingness to pay. Freight rates in shipping go up and down based on the number of ships and the demand for cargoes and securing higher than average rates in exchange for a lower probability of accidents is a difficult case to make according to the head of one fleet of product tankers.

Climate change

The oil industry's initial response to climate change was largely one of *denial* or perhaps *cover up*. In 1989 the Global Climate Coalition was founded by companies involved in oil and gas, coal, and automotive to sponsor, publish, and disseminate research that questioned the idea that man's use of fossil fuel was contributing to the greenhouse effect and hence causing the problem.

The organization began to break up in 1992 with Dupont leaving to become a co-founder of the World Business Council for Sustainable Development. BP left the group in 1997, as discussed in Chapter 2, and after losing Shell, Ford, and General Motors, the coalition ceased operations in 2002.

Perhaps the most pressing issue for the industry is the consideration of a carbon tax, which many *advocates* argue is the best way to mitigate climate change because it would encourage the market to move towards energy efficiency and renewables using pricing signals. The industry publicly opposes a tax but Exxon Mobile has, for example, built a $60 cost of carbon into its current "Outlook for Energy."

From an energy balance point of view, the industry is increasingly promoting natural gas as the fuel of choice for electrical power generation, as it does produce about one third less CO_2 than coal in a typical power plant. Natural gas was considered, for many years, to be an unwanted side effect of oil exploration and simply flared off. Flaring is still an issue for the industry and, although there are efforts to stop the practice, some countries still flare a significant amount of gas.

Many leading oil companies still do not publish sustainability reports or have not taken public steps to reduce their greenhouse gas emissions. BP does report such statistics and has reduced its emissions steadily since 2009 from 65.0 to 49.2 millions of tons of CO_2 equivalent in 2013.[6]

What the majors do is spend between 0.20 and 0.55 per cent of sales on R&D into both improving their abilities in oil and gas and looking into new forms of energy.[7] Exxon Mobil, for example, spends approximately $1 billion per year on R&D. One question is whether those spending levels will continue if the price of oil stays at the $50–60 per barrel level.[8]

Strategies

In terms of the strategies discussed in Chapter 4, the large international oil companies appear to be following a *wait and see* approach, as demonstrated by their large expenditures on R&D and their policy with respect to a carbon tax.

Although there are examples of *show and tell*, particularly on the issue of safety, the oil majors have not followed John Browne's very public approach when he was CEO of BP. One reason for this reluctance may be to avoid getting caught in contradictions if there is an accident in their very complex operations or if an *activist* does point the finger at their operations in a specific country or region, as has been done concerning Shell's record in Nigeria.

This issue is particularly critical for oil and gas companies with retail distribution such as networks of gasoline stations or domestic gas contracts, because the issue of consumer perception and behavior can be important as was demonstrated in 1995 during the controversy over Shell's disposal of the Brent Spar platform (see Box 6.1) in which public protests led by Greenpeace forced Shell to change its plans.

The majors, however, account for less than 15 per cent of the industry with national companies like Saudi Aramco, Pemex, and Gazprom making up about 80 per cent and smaller operators the rest.

National companies appear to be following more of a *low road* strategy, but may also be able to set their own rules in their countries. Small operators and so called "wildcatters," may even be tempted to *break the law*.

B O X   6 . 1   B R E N T   S P A R

A very clear example of how activists can attack a firm's license to operate is in Shell's 1995 experience[9] with its plans to dispose of the Brent Spar, a 14,500 ton buoy in the North Sea that had become obsolete when the Brent field was connected to the mainland via pipeline.

After a three year process with the U.K. authorities, it was decided that the best practical environmental option was to tow the buoy to deep water 150 miles west of Scotland and sink it. Although the Brent Spar had been emptied, there was still residual oil inside of the structure, which had been used to store oil produced at the Brent field while waiting to be shipped by tanker.

For Greenpeace, Brent Spar was and is a clear cut case of good versus evil. Its position is that "the ocean is not a dumping ground" and therefore any plan to dispose of an oil rig or ship by scuttling or sinking it is unacceptable. Greenpeace argued that Brent Spar had 5,500 tons of oil on board and would set a precedent for scuttling other North Sea infrastructure.

Greenpeace activists boarded the rig on April 30, 1995 prior to its demolition and managed to occupy it for a month. The film footage of the activists caused a media sensation in Europe and sparked a boycott of Shell by motorists. Sales fell in Germany by 20 per cent and some Shell stations reportedly saw a 50 per cent drop in revenue. Two service stations were fire-bombed and one was shot at.

While the British authorities supported their earlier findings that disposal at sea was the best option, 11 member states called for a moratorium on disposing of decommissioned platforms at sea, despite opposition from the United Kingdom and Norway. Shell eventually opted to dismantle the rig on land, clean it, and use it as part of the foundation for a new quay in Norway.

The total project costs would end up in the order of £60 million or almost three times the cost of the original plan as determined by Shell, approved by the United Kingdom, and confirmed by independent technical analysis. The 5,500 tons of oil that Greenpeace claimed were still on the Brent Spar turned out to be only 10 tons and, while Greenpeace acknowledged the error, it still maintains that the case was a win for the environment.[10]

Automotive

As of 2012, there were approximately 833 million cars and an additional 310 million commercial vehicles operating in the world.[11] Cars and trucks are, like energy, one of the building blocks of our society and personal, autonomous transportation has enabled people in many parts of the world an unparalleled degree of personal freedom.

The industry is made up of a relatively small number of large, integrated vehicle manufacturers such as General Motors, Toyota, Ford, Volkswagen, Nissan/Renault, Dongfeng, and others as well as a larger number of international suppliers who design and manufacture specific components. The industry is also supported by an even larger web of automotive retailers, petrol stations, repair shops, and other ancillary industries such as insurance companies.

Although the industry began in Europe and the United States, today it is a global business producing close to 65 million cars and 22 million trucks in 2013.[12] Taxes on new cars and gasoline also represent a huge source of funding for governments and the global industry employs tens of millions of people.

While the large environmental *activists* do not seem particularly engaged with automotive at the time of writing, one concern that is often discussed is what will happen as rates of motorization, or the number of cars per person in a given country, increases in the developing world. The prospect of eventually having 2 billion cars[13] on the road and the implications of that on traffic, safety, energy, and climate change are profound.

Two related issues are automotive safety and fuel economy, and in many ways the industry's response to these issues has foreshadowed its engagement with air pollution and climate change, which came later.

Automotive safety and fuel economy

Serious interest in automotive safety did not occur until Hugh DeHaven, a former pilot and researcher at Cornell University, conducted the first serious study of the second collision and, together with a colleague, invented the three point seat belt in 1952.

Ford offered seat belts in 1956 as part of an optional "lifeguard safety package" on one model, and Saab became the first manufacturer to install front seat belts as standard equipment in Sweden in 1958 and the United States in 1962.

In 1965, a lawyer, Ralph Nader, publicized traffic safety with his book *Unsafe at Any Speed*[14] that called attention to the tens of thousands of traffic deaths occurring each year and managed to raise enough public concern that national and state legislation was passed in 1966, which would eventually require cars to be equipped with seat belts.

With some exceptions, such as Sweden's Volvo, most manufacturers resisted the introduction of seat belts and also fought against air bags, which over the next 20 years, would become standard equipment on most cars and light trucks in the developed world.

The initial strategy of the car companies was to combine vigorous lobbying at the technical and political level with research and development in order to figure out how to comply with the new rules. The lobbying aimed to delay and dilute upcoming legislation arguing that safety improvements would add weight and cost to the vehicle, which the public was unwilling to pay for.

By the mid 1990s, the large car companies shifted gear and began using crumple zones and the number of airbags on their vehicles as a competitive feature as safety became one of the buying criteria of consumers following the process outlined by Noriaki Kano discussed in Chapter 3.

Fuel economy is typically measured in North America in terms of miles per gallon and in Europe as liters per 100 kilometers. The issue only became of general interest after the first oil shock in 1973, which tripled gasoline prices in the United States and gave smaller, lighter Japanese imports an edge in the U.S. market. In the United States, the federal government established corporate average fuel economy targets (CAFE) in 1975 for the industry, which called for doubling fuel economy over the next ten years.[15]

As they did on the issue of safety, the major car companies challenged the numbers and over the years have worked to delay increases to the CAFE standards, arguing that the consumer should be allowed to choose and that government has no business legislating technology. At the same time, the vehicle manufacturers have invested hundreds of millions in research into different ways to reduce weight and increase fuel efficiency.

Air pollution

While noise and traffic have been more or less accepted as by-products of our motorized society, vehicle manufacturers have been deeply involved in the debate about air pollution since the issue surfaced in Los Angeles in the 1950s.

California enacted the first air quality standards in 1959 and began a series of legislative requirements, which were intended to improve air quality in the state and in particular in Los Angeles. In 1967 the California Air Resources Board (CARB) was created and this institution, perhaps more than any other, would go on to lead the United States, and to a degree the world, in pushing the industry to adopt pollution mitigating technologies.

One of the key components of smog was determined to be nitric oxide (NO) and nitrogen dioxide (NO_2), which are emitted as part of an engine's exhaust and in 1970 the U.S. Congress passed the Clean Air Act, which set standards for car exhaust including rules for NO and NO_2 that would have to be met by 1976.

This requirement was met in 1975 by introducing a catalytic converter, which uses platinum, or other rare metals, to react with the exhaust and eliminate the NO_2 as well as carbon monoxide and other harmful compounds. One of the side effects of the roll out of catalytic converters was to also require the phase out of leaded gasoline, because the lead ruins the device.

In the 1970s the health impacts of lead on children were also discovered, creating a higher degree of urgency in phasing out leaded gasoline, which happened in the 1980s in the United States and Canada through complex negotiations between the Environmental Protection Agency and oil refineries. There has been tension at times between the automotive and oil companies as cleaner cars need different types of fuel and their interests do not always coincide.

The latest pollution issue is what are known as particulates and are the result of the combustion process in a diesel engine. Diesel engines are popular in Europe and are used by all heavy trucks because of their superior fuel economy. One solution is to equip vehicles with a filter or "trap," but that again adds weight to the vehicle, is expensive to produce, and reduces power to a small degree.

The technical nature of the air pollution and fuel economy issues have established a pattern in which governments use science to set the rules, the industry challenges those rules on a technical and political basis, and eventually compromises are worked out in terms of the timing and stringency of new requirements.

While the examples given here are drawn from the United States, a very similar process has happened in the European Union, Japan, and other industrialized countries.

Climate change

Over the last 10–15 years, European automotive manufacturers have largely been working on improved versions of internal combustion engines, which use less fuel and produce less CO_2 as a pragmatic and effective solution to the issue of climate change.

Many *advocates*, on the other hand, support the wholesale adoption of electric vehicles, which produce no exhaust and thus no air pollution at the tailpipe, although overall emissions need to include the source of electricity used (see Box 6.2).

Ford and General Motors have followed the pattern mentioned earlier and combined lobbying against further regulations with the launch of high profile electric and hybrid cars while Toyota has taken a different path, as discussed in Chapter 2, and is generally considered to be the industry leader in hybrid cars, of which it has sold over 7 million since 1977.

BOX 6.2 ELECTRIC CARS

Electric and hybrid vehicles are a growing segment of the automotive market, due partly to the perception that they produce less CO_2 emissions than cars with internal combustion engines. The degree to which this is true depends on the carbon footprint of the electricity used to power the car as well as the conventional vehicles that the electrics are compared against.

Complex models

If the power comes from nuclear, hydro, or wind energy, then logically the carbon is close to zero. France, for example, gets 76 per cent of its power from nuclear plants and thus electric cars in France will have a much lower carbon footprint than the same cars in Australia or China where coal represents 69 per cent and 66 per cent of the electricity mix respectively. A different energy mix will give a different level of CO_2 production per unit of energy.

It is also necessary to estimate the average electricity usage per mile or kilometer for a specific car and that, of course, depends on how fast it is driven, traffic conditions, and the use of air conditioning.

After that comes losses in the system, which include transmitting power across the grid, charging, and the so called "Vampire Loss" that occurs at stop lights. All of this needs to be added to the carbon produced in making the batteries and motors and that needs to be divided by an estimate for the distance the car will be driven it its lifetime.

In the end, the answer depends on the reports one chooses to read, which often use different assumptions and methodologies and reach different conclusions. Most reports give electric cars a significant advantage everywhere but in the heavy coal countries.

Holistic approach

One nagging question about many electric vehicles and hybrids is that most of them are equipped with DC brushless motors requiring high-powered magnets. The best magnets are made with rare earth metals that are mainly produced in China in reportedly appalling environmental conditions. An exception is Tesla which uses three-phase induction motors, which have no magnets.

The issue is that, when considering the sustainability of a specific product or technology, then a holistic approach should look at all aspects of the product's life cycle as well as the sources of its raw materials.

Several firms including Nissan/Renault and BMW have changed direction on the issue and embraced electric vehicles after first staying away from the technology; and it appears that other European firms are also changing their approach.

The other vehicle manufacturer that has had an important impact on the evolution of the electric car is Tesla Motors. Tesla sells about 20,000 of its battery electric sedan, the Tesla S, annually. Tesla's chairman, Elon Musk, is an entrepreneur who invested in the company because of his personal conviction that all cars will be electric in the future.

Tesla's strategy is to fill out its product line and reach 500,000 cars per year and is also building its own battery factory in the United States.[16] What has worked in Musk's favor is that investors have bought into his *pay for principal* vision and value the company at a little less than half that of General Motors, even though it sells less than 1 per cent as many cars.

Unlike Toyota's strategy, which considers different technological pathways and balances its development of alternative drive trains with the industry's leading internal combustion business, Tesla is a leap of faith and a throw of the dice. If Musk is correct, then there is a possibility that Tesla will become a brand as powerful as Ford or Toyota are today.

What Toyota has demonstrated with the Prius and the hybridization of its fleet is that there are consumers willing to pay for such technologies. Tesla has actually tapped into high-end customers who are willing to pay $85,000 for an all-electric vehicle despite significant tradeoffs in terms of overall weight, range, and interior space.

Strategies

In terms of safety and fuel economy, the automotive industry largely followed the strategy referred to as *wait and see*, which entails a combination of tracking the issue, using legal means to influence legislation, and at the same time preparing for tighter requirements and developing innovative solutions.

With respect to hybrid and electric cars as a solution for climate change, *wait and see* also describes the industry's response, including large investments in the technology made in the 1990s. Over the last few years, however, the companies have appeared to take a much more proactive stance and moved to *show and tell*. While there are large differences between the different firms, all have introduced hybrid models to the market and many have or will soon launch battery electric cars and spend a significant part of their marketing and PR budget promoting the vehicles and explaining their approach.

Ford, for example, has managed to displace Toyota at the top of *Fortune* magazine's 2014 ranking of green brands, which combines customer perceptions with a fact-based analysis, demonstrating the success of its *show and tell* approach.

There are exceptions to the rule. Toyota, for example, has consistently followed a *think ahead* strategy that is shown by consistency of its commitment over time and the breadth of models that are being offered across the fleet; and Tesla, which one could characterize as *Pay for principal* because the company has not yet turned a profit.

Fast-Moving Consumer Goods

Over the last 60 years, the consumer products industry has changed how we live, eat, and work and made our lives more convenient. Part of the process unfolding across the developing world today is the enormous appetite for consumer products that is growing as families acquire sufficient funds to buy into this lifestyle.

Most people in the West would agree that we are significantly better off than our grandparents, who had to work much harder to perform the most basic acts of everyday life. There is, however, an articulate but small part of the population, particularly in Germany, the United Kingdom and the United States, that calls into question the very structure of that society and feels strongly that we should go back to a simpler, more natural state.

Activist groups are targeting consumer products companies specifically because they do appear to be vulnerable to campaigns that highlight environmental problems of their products, operations, or supply chain partners.

The key issues that come up depend on the product categories in which companies are engaged. Food companies like Nestlé and Pepsico are very much involved in promoting sustainable farming and water conservation, while cosmetics firms may deal with humane animal testing protocols. Three issues common to all companies in the industry are environmental impact, packaging, and the efficiency and impact of their internal operations and that of their supply chain.

Environmental impact

To put the issue of environmental impact into context, it is important to recognize that many of the consumer products we take for granted were developed 50–100 years ago during the revolution in chemistry that was discussed in Chapter 1. Laundry detergent stands out as an illustrative example of how the industry has experienced and managed the issue and is explored in some detail in this section.

Modern laundry detergent has its origins in Proctor & Gamble's (P&G) invention of Tide, the first synthetic detergent, in 1933. In the 1950s, use of synthetic detergents in the United States, Europe, and Japan grew exponentially and its environmental impact became visibly apparent in sewage treatment plants, rivers, and even the open ocean when the water would become foamy due to residual chemical surfactants coming out of millions of laundry machines.

Regulators required companies to implement technical testing protocols to ensure the environmental safety of their products. P&G, for example, opened its Environmental Water Quality Laboratory in 1964 to study the impact of phosphates and cleaning agents on the environment and develop the science needed to design more benign products.

Although the change to biodegradable surfactants was achieved with relative ease, a much bigger issue was the use of phosphates in detergents and the impact that excess phosphorous had on streams and lakes.

Excess phosphorous causes plankton and algae to multiply well beyond their normal pattern, endangering natural ecosystems and impinging on human use in thousands of lakes around the world, including Lake Erie.[17] *Localist* organizations sprang up in different places as a result, and scientific and government attention was brought to bear on the issue. Canada passed legislation curbing phosphates in 1970.

The American detergent industry worked to shift some of the focus of its industry group, now called the Soap and Detergent Association, originally formed in 1926 for promoting hygiene, to researching the problem and lobbying. The worst case scenario for the industry was to face a patchwork of legislation in different parts of the country and one of the research streams of the association was to determine exactly how much of the excess phosphorous was really caused by laundry detergents.[18]

In the 1960s, P&G developed an alternative compound substituting phosphates with sodium nitrilotriacetate or NTA. The problem was that it was thought that NTA might cause cancer and, using the precautionary principal discussed in Chapter 1, the U.S. government would not allow the use of NTA until lengthy further testing was done, eventually approving the compound in 1980.[19]

By the end of the 1980s phosphates had been banned in a number of states, cities, and counties across the United States and the industry association eventually negotiated a voluntary ban on phosphate use in the United States in the early 1990s.

In Europe, the phosphate issue paralleled that of the United States. Henkel established its ecology department in 1953 and introduced its first phosphate-free detergents in 1977 using a mineral compound, zeolith A as a phosphate substitute. Henkel ceased all phosphate production in 1986.

The final twist in the phosphate story was the announcement in 2014 that P&G would cease all production of phosphate-based detergent within the next two years on a worldwide basis, as part of the company's strategy to be the leader in sustainability by 2020.

The legacy over the battle over phosphates was to make extensive testing of consumer products and life cycle analysis of them part of doing business, and set the pattern of scientific and regulatory engagement that has characterized the industry ever since.

Packaging

A second issue that is at the top of the agenda for the industry is packaging, in terms of the recyclability of packaging materials, their carbon footprint, and in the area of food products, their potential toxicity.

Europe has led the world on managing packaging and its approach has included both voluntary programs like the green dot program in Germany and regulatory action. Since 1994, the European Union has required member states to have a packaging policy and, in 2014, set an ambitious plan to recycle 80 per cent of packaging waste by 2030.

The green dot program is particularly interesting because it is managed by a non-governmental entity. Companies can choose to pay a fee to have their products certified as recyclable and consumers are free to choose those products over others. Perhaps the most interesting aspect of the program is that the fee is based on packaging volume and weight, such that there is a built-in incentive for firms to minimize packaging materials.

While in many ways Europe is ahead on packaging and recycling, the European Union has also passed food safety legislation prohibiting open bottles of olive oil and other condiments in restaurants and coffee shops and imposing minimum packaging requirements on farm fresh foods, thus increasing the demand for such materials.

Beverage packaging is an excellent example of the technological, regulatory, and market issues involved, which have shifted over time from returnable glass bottles, to disposable glass, tin plated steel, aluminum, and polyethylene terephthalate (PET) plastics and cartons. All of these solutions currently co-exist in the market and have different issues in terms of cost, consumer acceptance, and ecological footprint (see Box 6.3).

BOX 6.3 BEVERAGE CONTAINERS

The shift from refillable glass bottles of milk, beer, and then soft drinks to cans and other non-reusable packaging materials had to do with the emergence of large format supermarkets and the consolidation of the beer and soft drink industries, which occurred in the 1950s and 1960s, as well as technological advances in packaging.

The success of non-refillable cans prompted the glass bottle manufacturers to counter with lighter, cheaper, non-refillable glass bottles. Larger, high-speed bottling plants could fill and ship non-refillable containers at a lower cost to supermarkets than the local bottlers who used heavier, refillable bottles. As the tide tipped in favor of non-refillable bottles and cans, the economic model of returnable bottling collapsed as lower volumes needed to absorb the same fixed costs.

By the early 1970s non-refillable containers had achieved 60 per cent of the soft drink market and 75 per cent of the beer market in the United States and discarded cans and bottles were seen to be part of the larger issue of litter, which an activist organization called Keep America Beautiful had been formed to fight in 1953. In 1965, U.S. President Johnson's wife "Lady Bird" joined the organization and helped launch a number of successful campaigns to clean up the nation's rivers and highways.

These and other initiatives resulted in a peak in environmental awareness in the early 1970s and a push for recycling. In 1972, Oregon passed the first deposit law or "bottle bill" obliging retailers to charge a deposit on soft drink and beer containers, which would then be paid back when the containers were returned to the store. The idea is to make collection of the containers economical and thus support recycling.

Those states with such laws have seen sharp drops in litter partly due to the economic incentive of average citizens and also the possibility for underemployed people to deliberately collect discarded cans and bottles in order to receive the deposits.

In the early 1970s, the wave of concern for the environment helped the aluminum can industry replace glass and steel cans as the primary packaging for carbonated beverages and beer. Aluminum cans are lighter than steel and do not have the weld line, making it possible to paint the cans directly with attractive logos and product information. The aluminum can manufacturers also did an excellent job of pitching aluminum as being good for the environment even though other cans and bottles are also recycled.

Aluminum cans in turn were partially displaced by the more inexpensive PET bottles, which are lighter, allowed even faster filling rates, and had the benefit of being well-suited to larger, take-home sizes for soft drinks. The problem with PET is that, while recycled PET bottles can be readily used for making products such as carpets, recovery of the raw material for food quality use is very costly.

Over the last 20 years, the carton industry, led by Tetra Pak, has grown exponentially due to the low cost and technical characteristics of its packaging solutions, but also by making a sustainability argument, as all components can be recycled and the paperboard can be sourced from responsible forestry. Cartons are made on average with 75 per cent paperboard, 21 per cent polyethylene, and 4 per cent aluminum.

The toxicity of packaging materials is another issue and, in the last few years, research has shown that there is more interaction between food products and plastic containers than was previously thought. A specific component of many plastic bottles, Bisphenol A (BPA), is so close to human hormones that it can have a negative impact on health and particularly on children's development.

While the American Food and Drug Administration and the European Food Safety Authority have both determined that the level of BPA in food products is low enough to be safe, the European Union went ahead to ban the substance in baby bottles, because it is thought that microwaving the bottle could release more BPA into a baby's milk, and several countries have chosen to ban BPA in bottles, infant cups, and baby food.

Another relatively recent phenomena has been for the industry to recognize that its packaging is a major contributor to the overall carbon footprint of its products during their lifecycle. As companies increasingly have begun to measure the total amount of CO_2 produced by their products and services in line with the Global Reporting Initiative mentioned in Chapter 2, packaging has come under review. The Coca-Cola Company, for example, has found that the can represents 70 per cent of the entire carbon footprint of a Coke.[20]

A final aspect to the issue of packaging, which adds weight and materials, is the need to make products safe from malicious tampering of the kind that resulted in the deaths of seven people in the Chicago area in 1982 when a number of Tylenol packages were laced with potassium cyanide. Johnson & Johnson's crisis response, which was to recall all 31 million bottles in circulation, is considered a textbook example of sound crisis management. This case led to the tamperproof, shrink wrapped bottles we have today.

While the discussion in this section simplifies a very complex history, the key point is that competition between different packaging materials, which once had to do with cost, convenience, and the ability to put attractive artwork on the package, has increasingly also included environmental considerations in terms of recyclability, toxicology, and even carbon footprint.

Operations and supply chain

The third major issue that is of concern to the fast-moving consumer goods industry is the efficiency and environmental performance of their internal operations as well as that of their supply chain.

By and large the industry has embraced the idea of looking deeply at their operational footprint, because there is an almost direct link between increased efficiency and lower emissions of CO_2 and other waste products requiring expensive treatment or disposal, and if one looks at a collection of the sustainability reports of the leading companies, all have put programs in place to improve in this area.

A more challenging question is the management of a company's supply chain but two related trends have made this a particularly hot subject in the larger Western companies over the last few years. One motivation has been campaigns by *activists*, such as Greenpeace's attack on Nestlé concerning palm oil discussed in Chapter 3, and the other has been increasing attention on the part of very large retailers who are now using the environmental reputation of product manufacturers as a criteria to choose whether or not they will be distributed.

This last issue is related to the emergence of store brands or private labels in many product categories and the rationalization of the number of brands in stores in a given category. Many retailers now choose to have their own brand plus two or three other brands and the buyers are requiring companies to provide their own sustainability data and show that they have traceability back into the supply chain.

Strategies

As a group, the largest global consumer products companies such as P&G, Henkel, and Unilever appear to be following a *think ahead* strategy as they appear to recognize that the importance of their environmental performance to their retail customers and consumers will only increase with the passage of time, as will regulatory requirements concerning both toxicity and environmental impact.

Other leading companies in the industry are clearly following a very strong *show and tell* strategy and are exemplary in their effort to make sure that their internal processes and global exposure is consistent with the marketing message they are trying to convey.

What is less clear is the strategy of smaller companies and the thousands of private label manufacturers who do not have a direct relationship with consumers and are thus not as exposed to *activists'* efforts to change their business practices.

What both leading brands and private label manufacturers do share is increased scrutiny from leading distribution chains, particularly in the developed economies, as those firms do have a direct relationship with consumers.

The situation is very different in the developing world, where consumer products are growing very fast, and the issue about the differences in strategies in those regions will be explored further in Chapter 6. In general, however, one could say that the environmental awareness of the consumers in many developing countries is much lower than in the West and the cost pressure is much higher. Logically this would drive companies who are mainly focused on those markets to take more of a *wait and see* or even the *low road* approach.

Mining

As discussed in Chapter 3, the concept of the social license to operate was developed in the mining sector which has, over the last 30 years undergone a profound transformation in the way it sees itself and society. Mining is important because without coal, metals, and other critical minerals such as phosphates, our modern economy would grind to a halt.

While mining has been targeted by environmental groups of different types, the Chief Executive of Anglo American, Mark Cutifani,[21] maintains that global mining activities disturb less than 1 per cent of the Earth's surface. The issue is that mining has an enormous impact on that 1 per cent as well as the communities that live nearby.

Mining is also an interesting example because, although the issues are very different, the industry's development does track, to some degree, that of oil and gas; especially concerning the legal license to operate and the possibility that in the future mining rights will be exploited by national mineral companies, much like they are run by national oil companies today.

The issues in mining that have to do directly with environmental impact are mainly concerned with greenhouse gas emissions, water contamination, and land management. For the industry, however, more pressing issues relate to safety and the relationship between mining companies and the communities and governments around them.

Mining is often fought by *activists, conservationists,* and *localists,* depending on the specific project. It also can provoke different reactions from local people and can divide communities between those who want to or need to work at the mine and those who want to maintain a place's natural beauty and are concerned about contamination of rivers, lakes, and ground water.

Greenhouse gas emissions

Mining uses tremendous amounts of energy in the process of extracting, processing, and transporting ore. Like the consumer products industry, there is a direct relationship with energy efficiency, lower costs, and lower emissions and thus leading companies have been making improvement in these areas for the last few years. BHP Billiton, for example, has made the commitment to keep its total emissions of CO_2 at 2006 levels, even though the company is much larger today.[22]

Water contamination

Mining uses tremendous amounts of water to clean and separate minerals and in many cases the water is mixed with powerful chemical or natural agents in order to separate ore from the surrounding rock. Such beatification processes produce waste water, which is typically filtered and treated such that it is non toxic. It still, however, needs to be stored and thus most mines will, over time, create a tailings pond or artificial lake where the tailings can be placed and allowed to settle.

The issue is being able to adequately model the buildup of contaminates and the strength of the dams that hold the tailings in such a way that only clean water flows into local rivers and streams and that any heavy metals or other contaminates are well contained.

A recurring environmental problem for mining operations has been the collapse of the dams, for example, at Buffalo Creek West Virginia in 1972 and near the Doñana national park in Spain in 1998. While such events are rare, the impact can be catastrophic both for the natural environment and the company that is held responsible.

When the dam broke at Los Frailes zinc mine, located about 40 kilometers upriver of Spain's Doñana national park, more than 5 million cubic meters (1.3 billion gallons) of acidic water with significant levels of zinc, copper, cadmium, lead, and trace amounts of arsenic were released into the Agrio river.

While emergency response by the Spanish government and the Canadian mining firm Boliden managed to divert much of the contaminated water away from Donaña and the company insisted that the "park was not harmed,"[23] scientists have found trace elements of heavy metals in water fowl ten years later.

The cleanup cost the company and local government hundreds of millions of dollars and the problems at Los Frailes were reported to have been one of the issues that led Boliden to post losses in 1998 and 1999 and eventually to a deep restructuring of the company's portfolio and management team.

One research project identified 147 incidents around the world, which indicates, if one considers the thousands of mines in operation, that such events are extremely rare. The issue is that the failure of a tailing dam can be considered a catastrophic risk and can cause enormous damage, cost hundreds of millions of dollars to clean up, and has often resulted in changes to senior management, such as in the case of Boliden.

Activist organizations point to the toxicity of tailings and the potential risk as reasons to ban specific beatification processes outright, such as cyanide leaching for gold mining. The industry, naturally, opposes such bans and continues to engage in R&D to make the processes safer and to follow increasingly stringent technical protocols in line with government legislation.

Localist groups often oppose the water withdrawals needed to conduct mining operations, but their interests often conflict with other local political groups who see a local mine as a source of jobs and economic empowerment.

Land management and community relations

Although the most responsible companies will refurbish and replant the land they work, the fact is that modern strip mining methods destroy the natural landscape during the life of the mine.

A related problem is that mines are often located in remote areas and roads and railways must be constructed in order to get heavy machinery onto the site and to bring extracted ore to market. One solution for particularly remote sites is to build pipelines to carry ore suspended in water from the mine to its destination. This was the solution at Anglo American's Minas-Rio project in Brazil, which ships high-grade iron ore to a specially built port terminal 520 kilometers (323 miles) away. While less invasive than a railway line, the pipeline still crosses two Brazilian states, 300 towns, and required the company to obtain the right of way from 1,500 land owners.

Land management issues are often at the heart of *localist* opposition to mines and thus community relations has been one of the most pressing capabilities that mining companies have had to develop, which explains the interest in the social license to operate discussed in Chapter 3. Leading mining companies have developed very well-defined stakeholder engagement programs and routinely invest significant amounts of money in building community relations with local and municipal governments as well as civic groups of all kinds.

At Minas-Rio, for example, Anglo American used its own stakeholder management system to rebuild community relations, spending hundreds of millions of dollars on roads, bridges, schools, a medical clinic, and even a police station for the six towns located around the mine.

One interesting wrinkle in the ins and outs of such activity is the nature of political organization at the very local level and the long-term presence of a mine in a community. Mining companies will typically contact the local political leaders, such as the mayor of a town or village or county supervisor, in order to understand the communities' needs. At times, local elections will change the people in power and require the mining company to go back and re-start negotiations with different people who may have different political agendas.

Although not related directly to environmental impact, mine safety is a critical social issue and an integral part to a holistic approach to stakeholder engagement that the leading mining companies have all adopted to one degree or another.

Strategic options

With respect to environmental and social issues, most leading mining companies appear to be following a *show and tell* strategy, although some may be quietly going further in what is referred to as *think ahead*. The top five mining companies publish sustainability reports in line with the Global Reporting Initiative's recommendations and stress their efforts in safety, community involvement, and CO_2 mitigation.

Looking ahead, some mining companies consider the nationalization of oil resources, which occurred during the second half of the last century, as a very real scenario for the future of mining. As stated earlier, the oil majors actually produce less than 15 per cent of the world's oil and in many cases act as contractors to national oil companies who pay them a fee for their operational and technical expertise.

One mining CEO has set the internal goal of being the most environmentally and socially responsible company in the industry, partly with an eye set on that possible future. His vision is to go well beyond compliance in order to build the organizational capability needed to achieve competitive advantage in the future in a clear example of *think ahead*.

An issue in mining, however, is that smaller international operators and even large companies in developing countries may not adhere to the same strict standards as the international, publicly traded companies. A group of Chinese companies, for example, dominate the world supply of rare earth metals and reportedly have caused unparalleled destruction to the natural environment of Baotou in Inner Mongolia.

IT/consumer Electronics

The information technology and consumer electronics sectors are discussed together because of what academics would call their co-evolution during the last 10–20 years. As computing power and the internet have become more ubiquitous, the capabilities of our mobile phones and other electronic devices have continued to improve, changing the way we live, work, and communicate with each other.

All of these devices have power requirements and produce other environmental externalities that have increasingly come to the attention of *advocate* organizations like the International Energy Agency and *activists* such as Greenpeace.

One estimate is that the total energy consumption of the information and communications technology (ICT) infrastructure is approaching 10 per cent of the total electricity generated in the world[24] and, while other estimates are lower, the issue is one of concern as this sector is growing exponentially. This includes the data centers or server farms, which are the backbone of the internet, as well as the plethora of different devices needed to access that data and the telecommunications systems that connect everything together.

At the time of writing, the key issues facing the companies involved are the carbon footprint of their server farms and factories, sourcing issues that are mainly social in nature, and the recyclability or lack thereof of both consumer electronics and the servers running the internet.

Carbon footprint and climate change

The internet is made up of literally millions of computers, tablets, and smartphones linked together through an incredibly complex global network of fiber optic cables, routers, and other devices. Leading companies in the space such as Google, Facebook, and Netflix have huge amounts of computer power available and distributed in dozens of data centers, which use an enormous amount of primary electric power and require huge amounts of cooling to keep the electronics from overheating.

According to a 2012 GeSI report, the sector contributed 1.3 per cent of global greenhouse gas emissions in 2002 and will reach 2.3 per cent by 2020.[25] The major point of the study is not the carbon footprint of the industry, which it does recognize, but the abatement potential of the internet and computer-aided technologies, which the report estimates at ten times the sector's footprint.

Google and Facebook have taken leading positions on the issue of data center power consumption and carbon footprint, most likely due to a combination of the ethical convictions on the part of the founders of both companies and concern that their user base is very sensitive to the environment and thus that they are vulnerable on this issue.

Google claims that it has been carbon neutral since 2007[26] through a combination of energy efficiency at its data centers and offices, active sourcing of renewable energy, and investing in carbon offsets for the remaining impact. According to Google, one month of usage of their systems produces as much CO_2 as driving the average car 1 mile.

Facebook also has very efficient data centers, tracks its carbon footprint, and publishes the energy mix of the electricity it does use. According to Facebook, one year of using the site has the same carbon footprint as consuming a medium latte in a coffee shop.

One measure of data center efficiency is the ratio of all energy used divided by that needed to only power the computers. This is called a PUE factor and Facebook proudly announced that its PUE factor was 1.09 in 2013, indicating that its cooling systems are incredibly effective.

Neither Google nor Facebook discuss the energy needs of the devices that are used to access their sites, but the International Energy Agency (IEA) points at these devices as the primary concern going forward and is running a campaign targeted at the role of leaving such devices on standby mode all of the time. According to the IEA, standby power used 16 per cent of the residential electricity in the United Kingdom in 2012 and on a global basis will represent one of the largest opportunities to cut energy usage in the future.[27]

While such high-profile companies appear to be pursuing a strategy to go well beyond compliance in what might be a mix of *pay for principal* and *think ahead*, the concern of analysts is that there are literally tens of thousands of such data centers scattered throughout the world and not all of them are doing so much.

Greenpeace is paying attention to the issue and published in 2014 a second report on where the different companies are on the issue,[28] using data from the BCG's report. Greenpeace praises Google and Facebook, blasts Amazon for dragging its feet, and says Apple has improved greatly since its last report in 2012.

Apple is an interesting example because it operates a number of large data centers and is also a large manufacturer of devices including computers, ipads, ipods, and smartphones. Apple claims its data centers are 100 per cent carbon neutral and has built its own solar power arrays to achieve that target.

In terms of devices, Apple does not give specific consumption but it does design all of its products to achieve the gold level of EPEAT, which is a voluntary set of environmental standards used by the electronics industry. Other companies in the space, such as smartphone leader Samsung, also publish annual sustainability reports but do not address the power consumption and resulting carbon footprint of their products.

The study referenced in this section projects that powering devices will contribute 53 per cent of the total industry footprint in 2020.[29]

Sourcing

Sourcing for many electronics companies has to do with two different issues, which are more social than environmental but significant for the industry. One is the labor and environmental processes of the large sub-contractors who manufacture the computers, phones, and tablets that are sold under the international brands. The other is the use of specific components and minerals such as tantalum, which can be mined in regions currently experiencing conflict.

On the first issue the giant third party suppliers Foxconn and Pegatron have been found to have worrying labor conditions and violate the very clear standards that Apple, Samsung, and other similar companies try to enforce.

The *activist* organization China Labor Watch specifically focuses on the issue, because it is said that the miniaturization of consumer electronics, which has benefits for both convenience and power consumption, requires people with small fingers and the requisite dexterity to assemble the devices. Asian teenagers are ideally suited to the task and thus employed by these companies who, in their own struggle for competitiveness, may be tempted to pursue a *low road* strategy with respect to the environmental and social laws of the countries and territories in which they operate and to drop below the minimum social standards set by their customers.

The other issue is that almost all consumer electronics contain specific components made from tantalum, and other materials, which can come from war-torn countries. Tantalum is useful in making high-powered mini capacitors and surface caustic wave filters and the average smartphone contains about 40 milligrams of tantalum.

The issue of conflict minerals became a public issue in the United States after section 1502 of the landmark Dodd-Frank legislation was enacted, which requires U.S. companies to certify that they do not have conflict minerals in their supply chains. Tantalum is of particular interest as it is sourced from the DRC as well as Brazil, and Australia. In the DRC it is found together with niobium in an ore called columbite – tantalite or coltan has been used to finance the different armies in a war that has cost over 5 million lives.

All major electronics companies have undertaken efforts to certify that their supply chains are free of conflict minerals, although it is a complex issue because once the mineral is processed and the refined metal produced it is difficult to trace it back to the source.

Recyclability

Recycling consumer electronics and the equipment needed for server farms and corporate applications has become a hot topic in the last few years, as well as a business opportunity in its own right. All the major manufacturers have recycling programs in place and Apple, for example, maintains that it recycles 85 per cent of all of the devices it sells and offers its customers free drop off at any one of its 400 Apple stores worldwide as well as other locations.[30] Although Samsung does not report a percentage, it did recycle 355 thousand tons of electronic materials in 2013.[31]

The Canadian government has also put in place a program to recycle consumer electronics and such programs are becoming commonplace at the municipal, regional, and national level in the developed economies. Part of the motivation for doing this is to keep lithium ion batteries and other potentially toxic components out of landfills and other parts of the waste processing cycle.

A growing industry has emerged because of the fact that the value of the copper, steel, plastics, gold, and other metals in the devices can be greater than the cost of their disassembly and processing. One study estimates the size of the business at just under $10 billion in 2012 and growing to over $41 billion by 2019.[32]

A typical contract at the municipal level, for example, gives a recycling company exclusive access to the waste stream, which it then processes at no cost but with a profit-sharing model for the city. Some companies also add data security to the decommissioning process and this is particularly relevant for disposing of servers that might hold sensitive information.

Potentially worrying aspects of the recycling business are the occupational hazards to workers involved in the disassembly process and this is particularly worrying in parts of the developing world where worker protection is limited.

Strategies

As has been shown, some of the leading companies in providing consumer-facing services and products such as Google, Facebook, and Apple are clearly pursuing a *think ahead* or *pay for principal* strategy, or some combination of both. They recognize that their target markets are sensitive to the issue and have, most likely, determined that the cost of going well beyond compliance is a small price to pay within the context of their cost structure.

Others, such as number of the telecoms companies and even device giant Samsung, appear to be following more of a *show and tell* strategy, commissioning, for example, the GeSI report[33] cited earlier, which shows that the industry has a significant carbon footprint but offers ten times more carbon abatement opportunities.

The primary concern of *activists* and *advocates* in this case is, however, that the spread of smartphones and internet enabled devices, what is called the internet of things, will continue to follow an exponential curve and that new emerging economies may not put the same emphasis on the carbon footprint, sourcing, and recycling as do Europe, Japan, Korea, and the United States.

Conclusion

The five examples discussed in this chapter show how the strategic issues raised in Chapter 3 have had significant impact on companies in the five industries discussed.

The issue of a social and legal license to operate comes up in all five industries and tracks the waves of environmental interest discussed in Chapter 1. Events that occur such as oil spills, safety recalls, or other environmental problems are perceived to reach a tipping point, which raises public outcry. Environmental interest groups will do their best to influence public opinion and in some cases threaten the social license to operate of specific companies.

Legislation and regulatory oversight will then follow, as was seen in the case of double hulls for oil tankers, crash testing and fuel economy in cars, phosphates in detergents, recycling of electronics, and other issues.

The regulatory environment is typically very complex and can be influenced by scientific research, lobbying, and political pressure. Large companies typically respond by developing their own research capabilities both alone and in industry groups to try and bring their interpretation of the facts to the public debate.

Examples of firms dealing with catastrophic risk include the Exxon Valdez and Deepwater Horizon incidents, as well as specific cases of tampering with food products and over the counter drugs such as the Tylenol case. In mining, catastrophic risk can involve the failure of tailings dams.

While major players on the internet and in consumer electronics do not appear to have catastrophic environmental risks, the leading companies are taking steps to go well beyond the law's requirements in lowering their carbon footprint and recycling their products.

While it is still unclear if people will pay more for products and services they feel are more sustainable outside of the food category, companies with high exposure to consumers in the United States, Germany, the United Kingdom, and other markets are increasingly moving to *show and tell* as the consensus appears to be that consumer behavior can be impacted positively by doing more or negatively by being perceived as not doing enough.

Linked to this issue is the very fast pace of innovation spanning product categories, business models, and scientific research into toxicity and environmental impact. One of the interesting aspects of the rise of consumerist society in the second part of the last century was that it often developed in a decidedly unsustainable way. Looking ahead, innovation in all of the industries discussed often goes hand in hand with increases in sustainability and some firms have incorporated this idea into their planning. Henkel, for example, has sustainability criteria as an explicit part of its new product development process.

The last of the strategic issues discussed in Chapter 3, globalization, can also be seen to have an environmental aspect in the different industries discussed. Shell, for example, has worked hard to maintain its image in Western Europe but is now under attack for alleged sloppy environmental policy in its Nigerian subsidiary. P&G's recent announcement that it will cease using phosphates worldwide, despite their legality in many countries, is evidence of their concern that consumers will judge their behavior as global corporate citizens regardless of their compliance with local legislation.

While *activists* will pressure global companies to adhere to the highest standards in all of their operations around the world, the impact of that pressure may be to make companies uncompetitive compared to local players. International mining companies, for example, increasingly follow very strict codes of conduct on safety, community engagement, and the environment, regardless of the approach by local competitors.

As was seen in each of the industries mentioned in this chapter, there are important differences between different regions of the world and Chapter 7 discusses those differences.

chapter 7

Regional Differences

According to Pedro Videla, the chair of the Economics Department at IESE Business School, the headline in the history books for the last 10–20 years will not be about the internet or the 2008 financial crisis but the incredible increase in prosperity in the developing world, which saw an unprecedented 450 million people come out of poverty in the period from 1980 to 2010.

This period coincides with the rise of environmental consciousness described in Chapter 1 and these two trends, increasing wealth and population growth on the one hand and concerns about the environment on the other, are two of the key forces driving the unfolding history of the world.

This dynamic means that the relationship between business and the environment is and will be far from uniform around the world. The central issue is that as the developing world becomes richer it uses more energy, releasing more carbon into the atmosphere, and also generating all of the other environmental problems that have come into play in the West, such as air and water pollution, product safety, and managing the waste streams associated with consumer society.

Writing about inequality and wealth, economist Simon Kuznets found that the relationship had an upside down U shape and that people in both poor and rich societies were more equal than those from societies in the middle where inequality was higher. In the 1990s a number of researchers found a similar pattern in the relationship between economic wealth and environmental performance and this is called an environmental Kuznets curve.

While there is a debate about the validity of the idea and the strength of the mathematics that are used to support it,[1] the basic idea is compelling. Poor countries produce little environmental damage and then tend to use more energy and produce more CO_2 and other pollutants as they get richer. Eventually, the environmental costs becomes significant and wealthier people are able to focus more on their surroundings, implement political controls, and adopt cleaner technologies, which ought to be more efficient.

The construct is also helpful in comparing different regions of the world and the following section will look at it in the context of each particular country or region situation including its:

- Level of environmental surplus or stress in terms of energy, water, and other resources.
- Socio economic structure.
- Industrial fabric and the environmental sensibility of the companies in the region.
- Local and international environmental interest groups.
- Geopolitical situation and its situation with regard to the upcoming negotiations on climate change.

This chapter will thus explore these issues in the following different countries and regions of the world: The United States, Europe, China, India, and Africa. These five areas were chosen because they are exemplary of the issues raised in other parts of the world. As each one could be the subject of several books on business and the environment, the purpose is not to be comprehensive but to touch on the key aspects of developing business strategy in light of the environmental situation in each of these parts of the world.

The United States

The United States lies in North America and has a number of very different geographic regions. In the far north, Alaska sits on what geographers call the Canadian Shield and brings the United States into the limited group of Arctic countries. Hawaii lies 3,200 kilometers (2,000 miles) west of California, which is cut off from the rest of the country by the high sierras and Rocky Mountains. East of the mountains are the Great Plains and then the eastern seaboard. The southern part of the country is also geographically quite distinct from the rest.

Resources

The United States is incredibly rich in natural resources including oil, coal, and other minerals. The country is also relatively sparsely populated with only 35 people per square kilometer (13.5 people per square mile) and, while that number is an average of the different parts of the country mentioned earlier, it gives a sense of the emptiness of the land.

To a large degree, the history of the United States has been marked by its natural bounty, the space available for human expansion, and the features of the landscape such as the Rocky Mountains that separate the western part from the rest or the Mississippi river, which connects the Great Plains to the sea. The relatively high level of home ownership, for example, has been traced back to the frontier spirit and value in owning land.

The southwestern part of the country is, at the time of writing, enduring the worst drought in a generation and while the country is generally water rich, the local situation in parts of Colorado, Texas, Nevada, and California is very serious.

Population and wealth

According to the World Bank, the United States is ranked tenth in the world in terms of gross domestic product (GDP) and the U.S. Census puts median household income at just under $52,000.[2] A more complex picture emerges if one looks not at the average but the income distribution in the country, which according to Paul Krugman has become more unequal in the last few decades.[3]

One survey estimates that 21 per cent of American consumers are what it called "actives" or people who will modify their purchasing behavior based on their perception of a product or company's environmental reputation[4] and that these consumers are affluent, early adopters, and brand loyal.

The American market has the potential to become more environmentally sensitive as time goes by and largely explains the high level of interest by firms with significant interest in the United States to position themselves as sustainable. There are, however, regional differences in attitudes concerning the environment across the country.

The public's perception about climate change, for example, varies regionally, with the highest levels of concern on the east and west coasts.[5] In Alaska and the northern states attitudes are more complex as the evidence of climate change is readily at hand, but many people depend on forestry, mining, and the energy business for their livelihood.

A final factor to consider is that the United States has the highest energy consumption, per capita carbon emissions, and highest water usage of any other country in the world. The reasons behind the current situation have to do with American history and its relative prosperity in the decades preceding the current concerns about climate change and carbon emissions.

The country was growing economically and enjoyed energy surpluses up until 1970. Land was plentiful and the country's forests and water resources appeared unlimited. Thus sprawling suburbs with individual private homes were built and the private car became the primary mode of transportation. The current fabric of life emerged in the 1940s and 1950s when environmental issues were only just coming to light.

As was developed in Chapter 1, a significant part of the impetus for the wave of environmental activism in the 1960s and 1970s came from the largely affluent American middle classes who became concerned that their prosperity was being gained at the cost of the natural habitat. In terms of climate change and carbon emissions, Americans emit 16 tons of carbon per person per year and collectively produce about 15 per cent of global emissions.

Industry and its relationship to the environment

As discussed in Chapter 1, American industry was caught off guard by the first wave of environmental sensitivity in the 1960s and 1970s but has largely responded to the challenge, at least in terms of large businesses.

Since 2011, more than half of the *Fortune* 500 and the Standard & Poor's 500 have been publishing sustainability reports according to the GRI guidelines and, while the publication of such reports does not necessarily mean that a firm has fully embraced the concept of sustainability, it does indicate they have moved towards a *show and tell* approach.

The motivation for American companies to move beyond compliance appears to be largely generated by the interests of consumers on the one hand and activist shareholders on the other.

Environmental interest groups

Many of the world's largest environmental groups are located in the United States or are part of global networks with large American affiliates. The United States also has thousands of *localist* organizations who work to protect specific parts of the continent or to block specific projects.

Dealing with all types of such groups has become normal for U.S. firms over the last few decades and is largely managed by a growing cadre of professional sustainability managers. This is particularly true in businesses with a high degree of sensibility in terms of the environmental impact of the industries they are involved in, sensitivity of customer groups, conviction of majority shareholders, and perhaps the attention of some other stakeholder such as the local or regional government.

Political and geopolitical issues

In the United States there is an increasingly complex regulatory environment, which has grown since the early 1970s to cover many aspects of a company's environmental footprint. In the last few years, environment protection in general, and the issue of climate change in particular, have become political issues as well.

Federal law is relatively limited and most environmental legislation is done at the state level and varies between the 50 states. California typically has the strictest legislation on many issues, followed by the north east states such as Massachusetts, Connecticut, and New York.

One of the key issues for business, as shown in the example of phosphates in Chapter 6, has been to work towards clear federal rules and standards in order to avoid costly complexity by having to design and deliver different products and services in different states.

In terms of climate change, there are a number of very contentious issues in the United States at the time of writing, including the Keystone XL pipeline and the carbon emissions of the electrical generation industry. Keystone XL, which is mentioned briefly in Chapter 5, is a section of the North American pipeline network that is needed to bring oil produced from Canada's shale deposits located in Alberta to market via the Gulf Coast. Since the project crosses the border, it requires presidential approval and the pipeline has been converted by *activists* into a major political issue due to the fact that oil produced from shale has, on average, 20 per cent higher CO_2 emissions.

Natural gas, on the other hand produces lower carbon emissions than coal, which provided 45 per cent of the electricity production in the United States in 2013,[6] and, in a controversial step, the Environmental Protection Agency has mandated that states lower their CO_2 emissions over the next 16 years in electricity production practically obliging utilities to switch from coal to natural gas.

This ruling is part of the Obama administration's plan to live up to the landmark climate agreement it made with China, which requires the United States to reduce its per capita CO_2 emissions by 2030.

In political terms, these two issues reflect a broader split in the country between Democrats and Republicans and between states that support the jobs that the pipeline and coal mines provide versus others where voters are demanding action on climate change.

Doing business in the United States

From a business point of view, environmental sustainability has become very much part of the business landscape although there are variations at the state level. Most large companies are pursuing at least a *wait and see* approach as legislation will most likely continue to evolve towards greater environmental protection and interest groups will become more demanding over time. Many have gone further than that and some go well beyond compliance.

Europe

While the natural borders of Europe are often considered to be the Ural mountains to the east and the Mediterranean Sea to the south, for the purposes of this chapter, Europe will be considered as the 28 countries of the European Union plus Switzerland and Norway.

Northern Europe includes Scandinavia, Scotland, Ireland, and Iceland. The Northern European Plain is considered to go from the southern part of the United Kingdom all the way to the Baltic states and the Central Uplands that run up to the Alps, which cut the continent in half. Southern Europe stretches from the Iberian Peninsula to Greece along the Mediterranean coast.

Resources

Europe has a temperate climate and much of it enjoys abundant water and forests. Europe has little oil and gas outside of the North Sea but does have large amounts of coal in Germany, Poland, and Hungary as well as other European countries.

There is large diversity across the 28 countries and territories of the European Union and the issues are quite different, with some regions on the Mediterranean coast experiencing water stress and others in the East working to clean up a legacy of environmental neglect under communist rule. The Netherlands, for example, has a very particular environmental challenge and a highly developed environmental conciseness due to the fact that most of the country is flat and 17 per cent is located below sea level in land reclaimed from the sea.

Population and wealth

Population density also varies sharply across the region, with the United Kingdom and Holland enjoying the highest population density of the world and Norway one of the lowest. There are also wide disparities of wealth across the region and also within the different countries. GDP per capita was, for example, €25,700 on average in 2013 for the 28 member states but ranged from €83,400 in Luxembourg to the next highest, which was Denmark at €44,400, and the poorest, which was Bulgaria at €5,500.[7]

Differences can also be found within countries such as Spain, which is divided into 16 autonomous regions of which Madrid, Catalonia, and the Basque Country are the wealthiest and Andalusia and Extremadura the poorest with much smaller economies and high, endemic unemployment.

The complex and rich history of Europe is linked to its regions and nationalities and while the political ramifications will be picked up below, from a geographic point of view, different parts of the continent typically have different people living on them, or at least people with a different sense of their own history.

Thus if a major theme in a discussion of the United States is about the frontier and expansion, in Europe it is about a sense of place or what Roger Scruton calls Oikophilia or love of home. Scruton credits this sense to be at the heart of the conservation movement in his native

Britain and the fact that may European cities still enjoy an aesthetic harmony.[8]

Overall European attitudes about the environment also vary widely as do the specific subjects they are concerned about. Germans and Czechs, for example, are the most concerned with industrial accidents, while Cypriots and the Finns care more about water pollution.[9] The Green Dot program mentioned in Chapter 6 is considered successful in Germany but has not been rolled out across the region.

Despite these differences in geography and attitudes, the European Union has established standard environmental regulations across all member states, and thus created a complex situation because the legislative environment in Brussels is heavily influenced by wealthy Northern Europeans while many of the people in the South and the East are much more concerned with economic progress.

Industry and its relationship to the environment

In terms of environmental sensibility European companies tend to correlate well with their national roots and some of the most leading companies in the environmental area such as Unilever have their home bases in the Netherlands and the United Kingdom, while large firms from Southern and Eastern Europe seem to be taking more of a *wait and see* approach if that.

One of the key issues in doing business across Europe is that, while the environmental laws of member states are patterned on community law, the detailed legislation that spells out the legal requirements, inspection protocols, and legal penalties for non-compliance is still generated at the level of the different countries.

Generally speaking, Eastern Europe is well behind Western Europe in its development of environmental policy and regulations, but it also has a lower ecological footprint due to its relatively low levels of income and wealth. This creates a degree of ambiguity when determining exactly what it means to comply with all of the rules and regulations across the

28 member states. It is even more complex to determine what the costs of compliance are.

Environmental interest groups

Europe is also home to many of the world's leading environmental interest groups and both the United Kingdom and Germany were key to the rise of environmentalism in the 1960s and 1970s.

What is unique in Europe is the emergence of environmentally-oriented political parties that have even achieved political representation at the national and European level. In Germany the Greens achieved 10 per cent of the vote in the 2009 elections and the European Green Party has 50 members in the European parliament, that is, 6.7 per cent.

Part of the reason for the Greens' success is the nature of parliamentary politics in Europe where representation is primarily tied to a party's percentage of the vote in national elections rather than in small districts such as in the United States and the United Kingdom. By getting more than 5 per cent of the vote in West Germany, for example, the Greens gained access to parliament in 1983.

Another factor was the collapse of the extreme leftist parties and their adoption of the environmentalist agenda, which has created a very European thread of eco-Marxist politics.

While Europe does have a number of classical *conservationist* organizations and many *activist* groups, *localists* are also very active in specific places, as can be seen on the issue of hydraulic fracking discussed in Chapter 6.

Geopolitics and regional differences

European politics are exceedingly complex both at the regional and national level. In terms of the relationship between business and the natural environment, perhaps the most important phenomena has been the emergence of American style lobbying in Brussels over the last ten years.

The relationship between big business and European governments has been relatively close since the emergence of the present international order in the 17th and 18th centuries. As states grew in size and complexity, local companies also grew and in many ways a healthy symbiosis was created at the national level.[10]

National industrial policy was seen as a way to help industries succeed and often international diplomacy was conducted in order to open markets and provide access to raw materials for national champions. The European Union changed the situation by giving Brussels the power to break up monopolies, curb direct assistance from member states to particular companies or industries, and insist on "a level playing field" for competition.

In the environmental area, and in the related field of consumer health and safety, it has also created a regulatory structure where officials at the center pass legislation designed to protect Europeans and the natural environment but also can influence the competitive environment, for example by driving up the cost of compliance to food safety legislation such that only large, corporate farms can compete.

On the issue of climate change, Europe's progressive carbon trading system was hampered by the need to protect certain industries and eventually collapsed as a result of the downturn in European industrial production and over generous allowances for a number of industries. Part of the issue was protection against what is known as carbon leakage or creating a burden on European industry, which will make it uncompetitive.

The idea is that if you impose a limit on the carbon produced making bricks in Europe, for example, then the cost of making bricks for a European company will be higher than for its Chinese competitor, which has no such limits. The bricks would still be made and not only would the same amount of carbon be emitted but even more due to the shipping involved.

As a whole, Europe emits about 10 per cent more CO_2 than the United States but, as it does have more people, it currently contributes about

7.9 tons per person per year, which is much lower than the United States. The European average is made up of several countries, including Germany, the Czech Republic, and the Netherlands, which produce 9.2–9.8 tons per person annually, and France, Spain, Portugal, and Sweden, which range between 4.7 and 5.3 tons per person each year.

Doing business in Europe

From an environmental standpoint, the challenge for business in Europe is to deal with the uneven environmental sensibility across the different regions and segments of the European market and to accurately gauge the impact the issue will have on the consumer behavior of the different groups.

At the same time, the European Union continues to evolve and work out the balance between strengthening Brussels and European institutions and respecting the sovereignty of the member states. As the institutions gain more power, many companies are spending time and money both at the national level and in lobbying Brussels.

Finally, Europe's environmentalists will pounce on any sign that firms do one thing and say another or behave differently in different member states. For European companies, it seems the most viable strategies are either *wait and see* or develop a business strategy that allows the firm to go far out in front on environmental matters. As discussed in Chapter 4, this can be done by having leading shareholders who are willing to suffer the costs of such a strategy or by articulating a vision for the future that makes a positive business case for doing more than required in a number of markets.

China

In geographic terms, China is the world's third largest country, with an area of 9.6 million square kilometers. Over the last few years, China's economy has grown to rival that of the United States. China is also one of the oldest civilizations in the world and, with the exception of some of its more remote mountain ranges, has transformed the natural landscape perhaps more than any other place on Earth.

China's geography is dominated by the Himalayas and the Kunlun Shan mountains in the west, which support the Tibetan plateau. To the north lie the Talka Makan and Gobi deserts, sandwiched between the Tian Shan and Altun mountains. Most of Chinese history has occurred in the tremendously fertile plain that lies at the base of the plateau and runs down to the sea along its two major rivers, the Yellow and the Yangtze.

Resources

China is currently the world's largest producer of coal and the fourth largest producer of oil. It is also the world's largest importer of both commodities. China also possesses important mineral wealth including iron ore, copper, bauxite, and rare earth metals, of which China produces approximately 90–95 per cent of the world's supply.

In terms of water, China is currently building a $62 billion project, The South North Water Transfer Project, which as its name implies will bring water from the tropical south to the northern part of the country, which is suffering from long-term water stress because of population pressure on the Yellow river.

China's fast-paced industrialization has also caused widespread environmental problems in terms of water and air pollution and many analysts say that the country's ecosystem is on the brink of collapse.[11] Part of the process unfolding in China is the rapid expansion of its cities and the urbanization of its population. Years of economic expansion has brought hundreds of millions of Chinese to its booming cities and today 54 per cent of China's population is considered urban.

For Craig Simmons, a journalist living in Beijing, the even more critical issue is that China's new affluence is creating environmental problems well outside its borders by stimulating demand for coal, wood, and other commodities, adding huge amounts of CO_2 to the atmosphere, and kick starting the demand for illegal trafficking in endangered species, which are thought to have curative properties in Chinese medicine.[12]

Population and wealth

China has the world's largest population, 1.4 billion people,[13] and the economic reforms accomplished by Deng Xiaoping and his colleagues in the 1980s and 1990s set the country off on the fastest sustained period of economic growth ever seen. From 1978 to the present, the Chinese economy grew an average of 10 per cent per year and lifted hundreds of millions out of poverty, achieving all of the UN's millennial goals.

At the same time, China is still a developing country with GDP per capita at just $6,800 in 2013 and, while the growth is breathtaking, many people in China are still poor.

This increase in wealth was largely fed by booming industrial capacity in all economic sectors, which was initially built on exports but is increasingly being maintained by domestic demand for infrastructure and consumer products, especially in the growing cities mentioned earlier.

Since much of the country's wealth is located in cities in the eastern part of the country, one of the government's challenges is to bring economic development to the interior and western parts of the country. While China's overall population density is 145 people per square kilometer, this includes its overcrowded cities and much less dense countryside.

China's ecological problems are, in fact, very similar to those that the West has been dealing with over the last 50 years. The difference lies in the speed in which industrialization has taken place and the fact that China is only now starting to experience an awakening of environmental sensibility that happened 60 years ago in the West.

Industry and its relationship to the environment

During the last few decades, policy in China was subordinate to economic expansion and China's government is closely intertwined with the Communist Party and its state-owned banks, including the China Development Bank. The banks have been instrumental in financing the development of China's infrastructure, its state-owned enterprises, and the expansion of some of its leading companies abroad.[14]

Thus the relationship between Chinese industry and the environment is a very new one, which there has been very little focus on until recently. Chinese firms have largely operated in a kind of results-focused, laissez-faire world that has not been seen in the United States, Europe, or Japan since before World War II.

In many ways, China is a following the environmental Kuznets curve that was mentioned earlier and has begun the process of cleaning up its environment only as it has gotten richer. While China's first regulations on air and water pollution came out in 1983, China's Ministry of Environmental Protection was established in 2007 and China has enacted a new comprehensive environmental protection law in 2015.

One of the critical issues facing China, however, is that the new law relies on local environmental protection bureaus, which are staffed and funded by local politicians who may have conflicts of interest in terms of applying the law to large local companies.[15] Foreign firms working in China, however, need to be careful as Chinese officials may look more closely at foreign organizations. While there may not be the same level of inspection in general terms, high profile foreign investments may be more likely to be inspected.

The last point that makes China remarkable has been the tremendous speed at which it has been developing its energy, real estate, and automotive industries – all of which contribute greatly to the country's rising carbon footprint. China has also recently been developing its solar and wind energy sector, pouring investment capital into its leading companies and precipitating a worldwide crash in solar and wind prices as these companies seek export markets.

Environmental interest groups

While China has been the target for environmental interest groups from abroad, the government has not, in the past, tolerated the emergence of any type of large-scale environmentalist organizations. That being said, Edward Grumbine, an American environmental specialist in China, believes that public pressure is what led the Chinese leadership to make critical environmental commitments in 2014[16] and the new law allows

citizens, community groups, and NGOs to solicit data on the environment from the government.

There are also *advocate* organizations such as China's Energy Institute,
which is working together with the Rocky Mountain Institute and others
to map out a low carbon future for China.

Over the next few years, *localists* groups at the municipal level are
likely to emerge demanding cleaner air and water. The pollution level in
Chinese cities is horrendous by any measure and the issue is gaining trac-
tion amongst ordinary Chinese citizens. Wealthy people and international
expatriates, for example, can insulate themselves from the outside air
by living behind air purifiers and sending their children to schools with
domed sports and play areas, but this is not a luxury available to most.

Geopolitics and regional differences

As mentioned earlier, enforcement is a local issue and the central
Environmental Protection Agency acts only in an advisory capacity to
the local bureaus, which have overlapping authority with other ministries
responsible for water, land, agriculture, oceans, and forests.[17]

At the global level, China has recently signed a landmark agreement
with the United States to limit its carbon emissions to 10–12 tons per
person annually in 2030. This means that China, which is the world's
largest emitter of carbon, will continue to grow its emissions in the years
to come. In 2013 China was responsible for 9,977 metric tons of CO_2
according to the Global Carbon Project,[18] that is, 7.2 tons per person per
year. Raising that to 10–12 tons and allowing for some growth to China's
population would mean that China alone would emit 14–16,800 metric
tons of CO_2 in 2030.

Under the agreement, U.S. emissions would drop from their current
level of 16 tons per person per year to 10–12 and, again, if we assume
some growth to the U.S. population to 350 million, that would mean
3,500–4,200 metric tons or significantly less than its current 5,233 tons
and about a third of China's level.

One important issue is that as clear indications of climate change become visible at the planetary level, and many activists say that they already are, then China will come under pressure to reduce its emissions and may take some action. Given the strength of its central government, it is conceivable that China could move very quickly on issues such as electrification of its automotive industry, ramping up nuclear power, and so on.

Doing business in China

China has been in the process of the most ambitious and fastest economic and cultural transformation that the world has ever seen and the environmental legacy that it is creating will be felt in China and around the world.

The primary factor in that impact lies in bringing the standard of living of so many people up so fast and providing them with electricity, cars, and consumer products. On top of that, China has only recently started to put in environmental regulations and rules to limit the damage and conventional wisdom would say that the dissemination of cleaner business practices and renewable energy will take time.

China, however, may indeed implement far reaching legislation and adopt renewable technologies much faster than would be indicated by conventional wisdom. As of 2014, for example, China was already the largest market in the world for both wind and solar power and Chinese companies are quickly rising to leading positions in both industries.

In a seminar with 65 Chinese CEOs, only a few indicated that they were pursuing a *low road* strategy and a number of them explained why they were going beyond compliance. Western companies, in any case, are advised to go even further than Chinese law and operate in China as they would in the rest of the world. Chinese regulations and enforcement will catch up with the West in any case and activists are watching for signs of ecological dumping by western companies.

India

India is one of the world's largest countries, covering 3.2 million square kilometers, and is made up of 36 states and territories, which fall into five regions. India's north is dominated by the Himalayas and the disputed border with Pakistan in Kashmir as well as the Punjab and Delhi. In the north-east India runs all the way to Assam, which borders with Myanmar and Bangladesh.

Central India is known for the Vindhyachal Mountains, which essentially cut the country in two between north and south. Southern India is known for its tropical climate as well as Bangalore, Chennai, and Hyderabad. Finally, western India is built along the Arabian sea and includes Mumbai and the beaches of Goa.

Resources

In terms of water, India is considered to be relatively water rich as a whole, although large parts of western India, Rajasthan, Kutch, central India, and north Karnataka are prone to drought. Additionally, hundreds of millions of Indians lack access to reliable potable water and reports indicate that the country's aquifers are diminishing due to over withdrawal as a result of intensive agriculture.

India enjoys huge coal, iron ore, and bauxite deposits but little oil and gas and thus will likely continue to develop its energy infrastructure based on coal. Despite having its own reserves, India has been importing coal and has seen its mining output drop as a number of projects were facing resistance from *localist* groups for various reasons and also found to be in violation of environmental legislation.

Indian coal, however, has a high ash content and Coal India, a state-owned company that produces about 81 per cent of the country's output, is also considered to be very inefficient when compared to international companies.[19] In 2013, India imported 211 million tons of coal, that is, about 20 per cent of total consumption, and the current government is putting new plans in place to boost production and reduce imports.

Population and wealth

India is the world's second most populous country with 1.3 billion people and its population density is one of the highest in the world at 386 people per square kilometer.[20]

The economy in India has been growing very quickly since Manmohan Singh (finance minister from 1991 to 1996 and prime minister from 2004 to 2014) initiated sweeping economic reforms. While some say that India's progress has lifted hundreds of millions of people out of poverty, the numbers are contested and in any case economic prosperity is still unevenly distributed.

Another critical factor of India's recent development is urbanization. According to census data, India's urban populations have grown from 79 million people in 1961, that is, 18 per cent of the population, to 377 million people, that is, over 31 per cent, and continues to grow at just under 3 per cent per year.

Besides the split between urban and rural, India's population can also be segmented by income. India's National Council of Applied Economic Research segments the population into five economic groups as follows: At the bottom of the pyramid are people referred to as *deprived* or living on a family income of less than 90,000 rupees per year. Also considered poor are *Aspirers* who have between 90 and 200,000 rupees per year.

The middle class is said to include *seekers*, who earn 200,000–500,000 rupees per year, and *strivers*, who earn 500,000–1,000,000 rupees per year. An income of 200,000 rupees is equivalent to about $4,000 in terms of currency but buys about $23,000 worth of goods and services at purchasing power parity.

India's elite are referred to as *globals* and have annual family income above 1 million rupees or over $115,000 in purchasing power.

While Indian society strives to increase its economic wellbeing, traditionally, the different Indian peoples had a close relationship with the natural world. The indigenous Adivasi groups, for example, held many groves of trees to be sacred as are certain animals in the Hindu tradition. Since

1972, the Indian government has been managing the country's national parks system and conservation of tigers and elephants is thought to be very popular with the electorate.

In 1976, India passed the 42nd amendment to its Constitution, which made controversial changes to the relationship between the government and the Supreme Court but also stated that:

> *It shall be the duty of every citizen of India to protect and improve the natural environment including forests, lakes, rivers and wildlife and to have compassion for living creatures.*

Industry and its relationship to the environment

The relationship between industry and the environment in India was deeply affected by the Bhopal disaster in 1984 and neither the Indian government nor its people have accepted Union Carbide's claims that the accident was the result of sabotage.[21] As a direct result of Bhopal, India passed the Environmental Protection Act, which added to earlier legislation and gave new teeth to the Ministry of Forests – now called the Ministry of the Environment, Forests, and Climate Change.

India suffers from serious air and water pollution despite significant attempts to legislate improvements. India's Supreme Court, for example, imposed a series of action plans to curb air pollution in a number of cities starting with Dehli in 1996, but the city still has unsafe levels of air pollution because of too many cars and heavy trucks as well as the burning of crop residue in Punjab and Haryana.

The situation of India's rivers is also severe, despite repeated efforts to clean up the Ganges, which runs 2,500 kilometers (1,600 miles) from the western Himalayas across much of India and through Bangladesh before reaching the Bay of Bengal. India's current Prime Minister, Narendra Modi, has launched yet another effort to save the Ganges and appealed to the Indian diaspora for financial and technical assistance.

India is a mix of contrasts with respect to business and the environment. Large, high profile, Indian companies such as the Tata Group, Indian Oil, and Infosys appear to have adopted a *show and tell* strategy and publish sustainability reports with the latest GRI standards; but some are, at the same time, targeted by *activists* as being the largest violators of environmental law and community safeguards.

To make matters even more complex, much of India's economy is in the hands of small to medium-sized enterprises, which operate at a very local level and in the informal economy where there is little or no enforcement of environmental legislation.

Environmental interest groups

While India has a number of leading environmentalists and local groups of all types, there are also Western based groups active in India. In early 2015, there were reports that the Modi government is restricting the travel and finances of Western environmental groups active in the country such as Greenpeace, 350.org, and the Sierra Club.

A spokesman of Modi's ruling Bharatiya Janata Party reportedly said that environmentalists who are against India burning coal are "acting as foreign propagandists and foreign agents."[22]

Indian environmental groups are often connected to specific places or issues such as Siruthuli, which works on rooftop water collection in the city of Coimbatore; Exnora, which is focused on the environment in Tamil Nadu; or the Goa Foundation, which, as its name implies, is primarily focused on improving the environment in Goa.

Geopolitics and regional differences

Although India's carbon emissions are ranked third in the world behind China and the United States, total emissions are less than half that of the United States and about a quarter of China's. India's per capita carbon footprint is 1.9 tons of CO_2 per person per year and the issue flagged by India is that its per capita carbon footprint must rise sharply if it is going to bring prosperity to its people. Activists challenge this idea and argue that the Modi government is hiding behind the poor and that affluent Indians already produce European levels of CO_2.

The issue is that approximately 320 million Indians still lack access to electricity and supply is intermittent in the country at large. Despite a political commitment of the Modi government to bring 100 gigawatts of solar power on line by 2022 and to develop hydropower in the Himalayas, most analysts expect India to continue to increase its electrical output using coal.

India is also dealing with enormous ethnic, economic, and environmental differences across its own territory and an ongoing conflict in its relations with Pakistan. The border states of Jammu and Kashmir represent a particularly complex issue between the two countries and the local militants who favor an independent Kashmir.

With regards to China, the border has been tense but peaceful since China withdrew its troops from Indian territory after a brief incursion in 1962, but there is still a degree of tension between the countries due to China's continued occupation of Tibet and India's very public support for the Dalai Lama, who has his base in India and continues to lobby for Tibetan independence.

From an environmental point of view these tensions are significant because the region is connected by water basins and there is even more hydroelectric capacity beyond India's borders in the foothills of the Himalayas, which can only be harvested if there is a high degree of international cooperation.

Doing business in India

India, like China, is still focused on economic expansion but has, over time, built up a formidable amount of environmental regulations far beyond what would have been expected using the environmental Kuznets curve discussed earlier. While India also suffers from the same issues of local enforcement as China, the situation is a bit different due to the role of the courts in India and perhaps a deeper respect for nature on the part of its population.

The primary challenge for India in the years ahead will be to balance its legal and cultural commitments to the environment with the needs of its growing consumer society. As India's *deprived* and *aspirers* move up the economic ladder to become *seekers*, and as they and the *strivers* begin to enjoy the lifestyle of the *globals*, India will need more energy and hence will produce more waste and CO_2.

According to a local environmental journalist, the real challenge will be to get Indian industry to comply with the country's existing environmental legislation and to extend environmental protection to the informal economy. Leading Indian companies may adopt a *wait and see* approach as India's government is likely to remove or reduce environmental hurdles on business while India's courts push in the other direction. Multinational companies will be compelled to follow their own international standards especially if pursuing *show and tell* in their home markets.

Africa

Africa covers over 30 million square kilometers, which is about one fifth of Earth's land mass. In the north, the Sahara is the world's largest desert, covering 25 per cent of Africa and stretching across the northern part of the continent. The Sahel separates the Sahara from the rest of the continent and is suffering from gradual desertification due to endemic draught, intensive agriculture, and deforestation. To the east lie the Ethiopian Highlands, which are divided in half by the Rift Valley.

The center of Africa is referred to as Savannah and is home to the Serengeti and the Ngorongoro Conservation Area. The Swahili Coast is on the eastern side of Africa and runs from Somalia to Mozambique. Africa's remaining rain forests can be found along the Congo River and its Great Lakes Region dominates the center of the continent. Southern Africa is notable for its rocky mountains and the Cape Floral Region.

Resources

While it is generally held that Africa has vast mineral wealth, the facts are that Africa only has high concentration of certain minerals such as gold and platinum, and strategic resources such as tantalum, mentioned in Chapter 6. Bright Simons, a Ghanaian journalist also points out that, on a per capita basis, Africa is not so well endowed and, in fact, that most of the continent's mineral wealth is found in only four of the continent's 55 countries: South Africa, Angola, Democratic Republic of Congo, and Guinea,[23] although Botswana could be added to his list.

In 2010 Africa had 9.5 per cent of the world's oil reserves and 7.9 per cent of its gas, particularly in Nigeria, Libya, Algeria, Egypt, and Angola.[24] An additional 21 countries have oil, gas, or both and while pan African production is currently about 9 million barrels per day it is expected to rise to 12 million by 2020.[25] The newest fields have been discovered in East Africa and significant investment is expected in Uganda and offshore of Kenya and Tanzania.

Water is also of great importance in Africa and particularly in the Sahel and the northern part of the continent. An example has been the difficulties in reaching agreements between Egypt, Sudan, Ethiopia, and the other eight countries along the Nile, the world's longest river.

The first three countries recently agreed on ten principles to manage Ethiopia's Renaissance Dam and assuage concerns raised by Egypt and Sudan. Water and energy come together in an even more ambitious and controversial project to dam the Congo river in the Democratic Republic of Congo (DRC). The Grand Inga will add 40,000 megawatts, that is, one third, to the total generation capacity of Africa and the controversy stems from the fact that only 6 per cent of the DRC currently has access to electricity and much of the power will be sent to South Africa.

Beyond the Sahel, African countries tend to have sufficient water in absolute terms but are woefully unable to bring it to their people, many of whom suffer from what is called economic water stress or the lack of needed infrastructure to bring clean water and sanitation to ordinary people.

Population and wealth

Africa is home to over 1 billion people and the problem with water, and many other of the continent's challenges, is the endemic poverty of many Africans. While economic growth over the last years has been remarkable, per capita levels of wealth are still quite low with sub Saharan Africa GDP at $1,657. This figure includes diamond-rich Botswana at $7,315 as well as Burkina Faso at $684.

Thus one of the myriad challenges for governments is to build a tax base that can pay for the necessary infrastructure and these types of projects are often caught in a web of highly local relationships and obligations, which adds costs to projects and allows corruption to delay social progress.

The largest economies on the continent are those of Nigeria, South Africa, and Egypt and on a per capita basis the richest countries are Gabon, Libya, Botswana, and South Africa as well as Mauritius and Equatorial Guinea.

The growth in African economies has also lifted millions of people out of poverty and added trillions to the continent's economy as a whole. At issue, however, is that most of the continent still appears to be below the level at which environmental concerns will begin to outweigh interest in material progress and, in fact, the rise of a consumer society will add increased stress to the environment, particularly in urban areas.

Urbanization in Africa is also increasing and the percentage of urban versus rural population is projected to continue to increase from just below 40 per cent in 2010 to 60 per cent by 2050, according to the United Nations. Of concern is that the trend to urbanization will largely occur in the sprawling informal settlements or slums such as Kibera in Nairobi. Life in such places can be extremely difficult and may, in fact, become more so as crowding and economic water stresses add to the pressure.

Industry and its relationship to the environment

With the notable exception of South Africa, environmental concerns do not appear to be particularly high on the radar of many African industries and governments as the continent is largely at the poor end of the environmental Kuznets curve.

To make the situation even more complex, the actual regulations in many African countries differ and enforcement is thought to be uneven, arbitrary, and lax. Ownership and the governance of many large companies in certain countries are also deeply connected to the political leadership, thus creating opportunity for collusion.

While it is likely that regulations and enforcement will increase over time, in the near term the strategic issue that will drive a higher level of environmental awareness will most likely be the issue of globalization discussed in Chapter 3.

Globalization is playing a double role in the context of African industry today. On the one hand, international companies doing business in Africa are finding that their environmental performance in African countries is of interest to *activists* back home. Shell, for example, has come under criticism for its seemingly lax environmental record in Nigeria. Companies that source raw materials or products from Africa face similar pressures.

The other dynamic starting to come into play is that African companies are increasingly expanding beyond Africa, either in terms of geographic footprint or in terms of shareholders. Those companies will find that their environmental sensibility will increase as their new customers and owners require them to have impeccable environmental credentials.

Environmental interest groups

The key to understanding the landscape of environmental interest groups in Africa is to distinguish between local, grassroots organizations and international interest groups that are active in Africa or have the continent as their primary area of focus.

While generalization is always dangerous, local organizations appear to be focused more on improving the lives of the people of Africa, for example, by working on programs to improve the productivity of small farmers and build out infrastructure for water and sanitation. Examples of such organizations include the African Conservation Tillage Network and The African Civil Society Network on Water and Sanitation.

The internationally based organizations, on the other hand, tend to be more focused on protecting African wildlife and its natural spaces from the development of African society itself, although all such groups make the case that conservation and economic development can go hand in hand.

One example of this last group is the African Wildlife Organization which is based in Washington D.C., has a $22 million budget, and is focused on conserving and protecting large animals such as elephants, lions, and so on. Founded in 1961 as the African Wildlife Leadership Foundation, the organization initially focused on education helping to establish the College of African Wildlife Management in Tanzania, a conservation education center in Kenya, and financing African scholars to gain higher degrees in the United States.

By 2014 the organization had field offices in Kenya, Zambia, Tanzania, and the DRC and is led by Patrick Bergin who has, since 2002, managed to triple the organization's budget and got into the eco-tourism business with a number of eco-lodges and photo safaris.

NGOs have been increasingly becoming the focus of international aid organizations, Western governments and the United Nations, as there is a sense that these organizations are a more reliable way of bringing money to bear on different types of problems than transferring funds to African governments.

Geopolitics and regional differences

Africa suffers from acute regional tensions over water rights, access to valuable minerals, and a host of tribal and regional issues left over from its colonization in the 19th century and very rapid de-colonization in the 1950s and 1960s. These conflicts, and potential conflicts, include the ongoing struggle in the Democratic Republic of Congo, the civil war in Libya, and the future of the Nile.

To make matters even more complex, Africa is also suffering at the hands of terrorist groups such as Boko-Haram in Northern Nigeria, which threaten to destabilize some of the nation states on the continent. Others such as Somalia have effectively ceased to function and are referred to as failed states.

Africa as a whole is highly susceptible to local and global climate issues and the combination of an increasing population with endemic poverty adds to environmental issues such as deforestation, which in turn creates higher environmental stress. While the conflicts mentioned here are political in nature, many have also been linked to environmental stress and some forecasters predict the situation will get worse over the next 40 years.[26]

On the environment, African countries agreed on the first pan African environmental agreement, The African Convention on the Conservation of Nature and Natural Resources, in Algeria in 1966 and then revised it in Maputo in 2003. However, only 30 African states have ratified the revised Convention and their implementation of it is thought to be "lukewarm" by the author of a study of the agreement.[27]

In terms of global climate discussions, the fact that Africa only contributes 3–4 per cent of global CO_2 emissions and has a per capita footprint of 1.1 tons of CO_2 per person per year, indicates that Africa will be able to pursue its economic expansion without interference for the foreseeable future.

Doing business in Africa

Africa and its development will have a huge impact on the natural environment as it begins to industrialize, because there are enormous business opportunities across Africa involving infrastructure development, in many cases financed by China, and consumer society. These opportunities will be pursued by local companies with potentially little environmental sensibility and in a relatively lax regulatory environment in many countries.

Thus doing business in Africa will be complicated for Western firms hampered by their need to present a uniformly clean image in their global operations. Compared to local and Chinese companies pursuing a *low road* approach at best, Western companies may find themselves at a competitive disadvantage unless they risk creating an opportunity for *activists* to embarrass them by claiming that they follow a double standard.

Conclusion

As seen in this chapter's discussion of five different parts of the world, the environmental issues are different in each place and have to do with the geography, social dynamics, and politics of each region.

In terms of environmental sensibility, Europe is, in many ways, ahead of the United States, which in turn is far ahead of China, India, and Africa. While the best recommended strategy for a specific company depends on the industry it is in and its ownership structure, some general recommendations can be made.

For large companies involved in Europe and the United States, which are either publicly traded or highly visible with the general public, it seems that the minimal approach ought to be pursuing a *show and tell* strategy, at least to some degree. The problem with that approach is that it will eventually require the firm to apply similar environmental standards in other global markets, such as those in China, India, and Africa, where their local competitors will not be required to do so.

Large Chinese and Indian companies may see environmental regulations increase due to moves by the Chinese government, on the one hand, and the Indian courts, on the other, to intervene and push for greater compliance with current and future environmental regulations. For this reason, *wait and see* appears to be the minimal recommended course, although for those firms becoming active in the West, a higher degree of activity, or at least the appearance of it, will be required by Western industrial customers and consumers.

Although there will be exceptions in those African countries, such as South Africa and Kenya, with relatively robust court systems, most African companies will probably adopt a *low road* approach. What this means for companies with a global footprint is that it may become increasingly difficult to compete in Africa if the organization feels it must impose Western environmental standards on its African operating units. An exception to this might be firms based in the Middle East, China,

India, and other countries where there will be little pressure from consumers, shareholder, or regulators in the home markets.

One region of the world, the Arctic, will prove a test bed for how these global trends will play out, as firms from a number of countries will be involved in developing its economic potential despite its extremely delicate ecological situation (see Box 7.1).

BOX 7.1 THE ARCTIC

The Arctic is normally considered to be the region of the world above 66°32'N Longitude. While the Arctic comes under the authority of the Law of the Sea, an organization called the Arctic Council was founded in 1996 in order to provide a forum for the Arctic states, which include Canada, Denmark (which also includes Greenland), Finland, Russia, Sweden, and the United States. China, as well as a number of other countries and NGOs, has observer status.

Climate change is being felt very clearly in the Arctic; the amount of summer ice is dropping faster than many models predicted and according to NASA reached a minimum in 2012. Besides enormous impact on the people and animals in the region, it also presents huge business opportunities including the development of the Arctic's natural resources and shipping.

The Arctic region's potential for oil, gas, and a wide range of minerals is enormous, although compared to other parts of the world it is largely unexplored and not confirmed.

The issue, according to Pano Kroko, the President of the Environmental Parliament, is that as it becomes possible to access the Arctic three to four months per year, then it will become increasingly economically viable to exploit its mineral wealth and more and more important to protect its social and ecological wealth.

In 2014 Greenland's parliament voted to allow uranium mining for the first time and also gave permission for a new iron ore mine in the country, highlighting that the next big play in the world of mining and oil exploration may be the Arctic. In a 2008 report, the United States Geological Survey estimated 90 billion barrels of oil and 1,669 trillion cubic feet of gas north of the Arctic Circle, with 84 per cent of that offshore.

The other main impact of the decreasing ice is the opening up of the Arctic for shipping. Today, shipping to and from China and Japan to Europe involves a long trip and often means navigating either the Suez or the Panama Canal.

There are two Arctic alternatives. One route cuts across Northern Canada and Alaska, normally called the North–West passage. The other crosses Northern Russia and Siberia and is usually referred to as the Northern Sea Route. Both have the potential to cut weeks off the shipping time between East and West.

Since the first voyage of a LNG tanker, the OB River successfully made the trip from Hammerfest Norway to Tobata Japan in 2012, Russia has been actively promoting the Northern Sea Route and has given permits to hundreds of ships to make the trip with the obligatory escort of Russian Icebreakers. In the summer of 2014, the first Chinese ship, the Yong Shen, made the trip from Dalian in Southern China to Rotterdam via the Northern Sea Route reportedly shaving 13–15 days off the time through the Suez Canal.

One question raised by Kroko is how to manage this booming Arctic development in a way that protects its fragile environment and the people who live there. Western companies will be held accountable for their approach to the region but it is less clear what will stop Chinese and Russian firms from cutting corners on environmental protection.

$\begin{smallmatrix}\text{chapter}\end{smallmatrix}$ 8 What to Do?

Using the language of business and being firmly grounded in the assumptions and values of business leaders, the preceding chapters have endeavored to outline a business-oriented way of looking at the issue of environmental sustainability.

Chapter 1 explored those assumptions and values and showed how business was caught off guard by the waves of environmental concern and subsequent regulation, which began in the West but is spreading around the world. Chapter 2 discussed the way business reacted to these waves of environmentalism in the past and Chapter 3 teased out six strategic issues in which a firm's approach to the environment can have material impact on the business.

Chapter 4 then put forward possible strategic responses and introduced the idea of *environmental sensibility* as a way of classifying different companies in different industries and regions of the world. After discussing environmental interest groups and the role they play in Chapter 5, Chapters 6 and 7 gave examples of how these issues fit together in a number of industries and regions.

This chapter uses the ideas developed throughout the book and spells out how to apply them to a specific firm. The chapter goes through a framework that can be used to determine the best strategy to pursue and gives recommendations as to how to implement that strategy.

The framework is not conceptually complex but does require a serious effort to work through the different issues involved and do the analysis that is required. The next section goes back to the issue of corporate governance and stresses the importance of involving the company's board of directors in the process such that it supports the direction and is fully informed about the tradeoffs and risks inherent with it.

The third section of the chapter highlights four aspects of strategy implementation that are particularly critical in the area of sustainability and the chapter concludes with the importance of communications and training for different audiences, which ought to be designed.

Do the Math!

The title of this section is deliberate in that the ideas developed up to now can involve enormous complexity when one tries to make them operational. One of the premises of this book is, however, that there are no easy answers and that working through these concepts will take some time and effort.

As discussed in Chapter 3, the mathematics of environmental sustainability can be arduous since it is difficult to accurately model complex systems. Nevertheless, the task can be done and the good news is that the role of senior management is to direct the process and participate in defining assumptions and boundary conditions so that specialists can undertake the detailed calculations.

Review the past

The first step in the analysis is to recognize how the passage of time affects the issues at play and how a firm's future options are, to some extent, conditioned by its past and present. Academics call this phenomenon *path dependency*, but it is nothing more than the idea that we are where we are because of where we have been and that our next steps are conditioned, in part, by our last.

Thus the first step in developing a strategic approach to environmental sustainability is to develop an honest assessment of how the firm has responded to the environment in the past. Did the firm respond to the first or second wave of environmental activity with *denial* as developed in Chapter 2? Did it engage in any kind of *cover up* during its history? Such reflection can be painful for an organization, even if the executives responsible are no longer with the firm. It is, however, critical to understand where one is starting from.

Recognizing the history of large tobacco companies with regards to product safety, for example, Japan Tobacco International's former CEO, Pierre de Labouchere, strove to make the company, which markets Winston, Camel, and a number of other brands outside the United States, the most credible tobacco company in the world. His positioning and the effort that it required in the firm's research and marketing departments were the direct result of tobacco's history and won the respect of its employees, suppliers, and customers.

Has the firm gone through a crisis that has defined it and touched the lives of managers and employees? In some cases the crisis may have happened in the distant past but is still remembered by senior members of the management team and thus will have an effect on their behavior and possibly their performance.

If the firm has undertaken extensive *environmental PR* in the past it may be beneficial to go out in the marketplace and try to evaluate to what degree industrial customers and consumers feel this effort was genuine, or if there is a sense that the company was engaged in some kind of greenwashing.

Finally, if the firm attempted to genuinely engage with environmental interest groups in the past, or even went beyond *engagement* to *transformation and renewal*, it will be enormously helpful to accurately look at the success or failure of those efforts and, to the degree possible, quantify the costs and benefits associated with them.

Part of the reason that looking deeply into the company's past is so important is that the present culture of the firm will reflect what the organization has learned from its own past. In some cases, the prevailing wisdom of what worked and what did not work might not actually coincide with the facts, thus creating an important communications challenge before any change is even possible.

Besides looking at the firm itself, it is also useful to understand where the industry as a whole is coming from as well as looking at regional issues in the markets the firm operates in and the role environmental interest groups have played in these developments.

Understand the present

After understanding the past, the next step is to understand the present and to drill down on where the company is today in terms of compliance and the cost of that compliance.

For firms currently producing sustainability reports according to GRI's G3 or G4 guidelines, the current situation should be well documented. For those that have not yet begun to publish such reports, the magnitude of the task of figuring out the actual environmental footprint of every operating unit should not be underestimated.

What can be even more time consuming is to accurately estimate the abatement costs involved in achieving a specific environmental footprint, including the not inconsiderable cost of developing sustainability reports to the level of the guidelines. While there is ample evidence that efficiency gains can improve environmental performance on some aspects such as the relationship between carbon emissions and energy costs, reducing levels of air and water pollution often add costs to a firm's operations.

Once the baseline is well understood, it is then useful to review the current state of play in the industry, the region, and the behavior of environmental interest groups, which affect the company and potentially its suppliers and customers.

The first task is to compare the organization's performance with current regulation in the different places in which it operates to assure compliance across the board. The next step is to compare the level of performance between different operations in order to evaluate if there may be exposure to charges of ecological dumping, regardless of the legality of that performance. The cost of bringing all of a large, international firm's operations to some minimal standard level could be considerable and such a decision should not be taken lightly.

A different question is to determine the position of the entire organization relative to its competition in general and specifically in the different regions and territories in which it operates. Again, this is a complex undertaking, but is the only way to determine if local players are operating at a cost advantage due to a minimal approach to compliance or even malfeasance.

The final issue to look at is the current focus of environmental interest groups with respect to the firm's activities and that of its suppliers and customers. The example of Nestlé being attacked by Greenpeace for its purchases of palm oil, mentioned in Chapter 3, is an example of the kind of issue that could be uncovered through deep analysis.

Food manufacturers such as Nestlé had been using palm oil for years and; in fact, Greenpeace first attacked Unilever in April 2008 and the Kit Kat attack did not happen until March 2010. Nestlé used limited amounts of palm oil in its products and was a member of a group called the Round Table on Sustainable Palm Oil. What it had not done was to investigate its own suppliers or consider that Greenpeace could target Nestlé after reaching concessions from Unilever.

Making a full assessment of a large firm such as Nestlé or one of its product groups is an arduous undertaking but can prove its value if a major crisis can be avoided.

See the future

Once the past and present are well understood, it is possible to look ahead and explore what the future may bring. For this effort it is recommended to develop different scenarios for the different regions and territories in which the firm operates. Alternative scenarios are preferable to forecasts because predicting the level of future environmental concerns of the general public and the behavior of regulators with any degree of accuracy is difficult at best.

An example of the complexity is the ongoing process of climate talks that have gone on since the United Nations agreed on the Framework Convention on Climate Change in 1992. The signatories to the Convention have held a series of meetings all over the world and come to some agreements, such as the Kyoto Protocol. The issue is if and when the convention will agree on global standards for greenhouse gas emissions and what the timetable and enforcement mechanisms will be.

Adding to this complexity is the evolution of technological change at the industry level, which can greatly affect the environmental footprint of a given firm. Coupled with this are consumer and customer attitudes with respect to these issues. Electric vehicles are an example of technological change that can affect the automotive industry's future, depending on a wide variety of developments of technology, government regulations, and consumer behavior and preference. Electric vehicle sales are also influenced by the price of conventional fuel, which needs to be considered as part of the scenarios.

The final piece of the puzzle is to try and gauge what the priorities of environmental interest groups will be in the years ahead at the regional and industry level.

Putting all of these factors into two or three robust scenarios with a 10–20-year time horizon is the best way to stress test a firm's current strategy and to build the business case to either continue on the present course or take steps toward a different approach. Typically scenarios will plot higher and lower levels of environmental sensibility on a wide variety of issues.

Bringing it all together

Figure 8.1 shows the essential elements of the framework discussed in this chapter, which involve looking at the past, present, and future across

	Past	Present	Future
Region (s)			
Industry Segments			
Interest Groups			
Company / Firm			

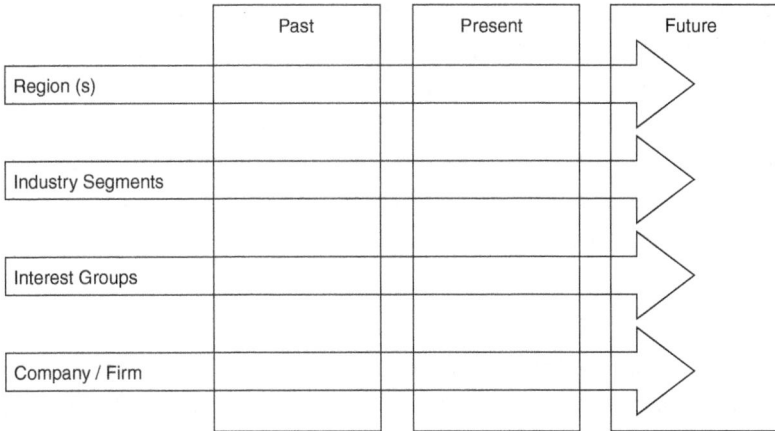

FIGURE 8.1 / Framework for Strategic Analysis

the region in which a firm is operating; its industry, customers, and suppliers; the types of interest groups that are active on the issues arising from its activities; and the firm itself.

For companies involved in different industries and regions, the analysis needs to be done for each individual component and subsequently brought together. Finding a common strategy, which is appropriate for all units of a large firm, may not be possible and the consideration of whether to allow different units to take different paths might be necessary.

Get the Board On Board

As discussed in Chapter 1, there are different approaches to corporate governance around the world, but inevitably there is a body of people who are responsible for maximizing shareholder value of a firm over time. Also, while the exact definition of the roles and responsibilities of the board as opposed to the CEO and management team might vary, it is widely accepted that the board needs to be involved with issues that can have a material impact on the future and, therefore, the value of the firm.

As this book has endeavored to show, environmental sustainability and the strategic issues that it affects have the potential to determine the success and failure of many firms over time and thus should be subject to board supervision. The fact that such issues have this potential supports the argument that boards have a fiduciary responsibility to at least look into the issues and determine to what extent they are or are not material to the future of the firm.

Strategic choices

The last point raised in the previous section, for example, deals with the choice facing a large, diversified company when its different operating units may actually benefit from different strategic options as defined in Chapter 4. One can, for example, imagine a company operating in two different business areas that are also located in different regions of the world. In this simplistic example, one might find the environmental sensibility of a firm in the North American energy sector to be quite high, while the mining business in an African country still operates more or less below the radar.

The question then becomes: Should the firm adopt a strategy that goes beyond compliance in its energy division but pursue a *low road* strategy in its mining arm? If this decision is left to the executive responsible for the mining division the answer will be clear. The CEO will also be tempted to follow such a path as the competitiveness of the mining division may be affected if it goes too far and thus the short-term profitability of the company could suffer.

At issue is the possibility that the situation in Africa changes or that *activists* link the company's performance in its different units causing embarrassment, scandal, or worse. Only the representatives of the company's owners can make the call on either taking the risk or paying the cost to bring its mining division up to an international standard of compliance, which might be far above that required by local regulators.

Even the case that a company only has one operating unit or that the situation is similar between different units poses a serious question.

Should the company get out in front on environmental sustainability or take a more reactive view? What the history of the corporate response to these issues shows is that firms ought to make rational choices and not be caught off guard as so many were in the past.

Build in or Buy In

Iris Firstenberg lectures at the Anderson School of the University of California, Los Angles and distinguishes between the ideas of *build in* and *buy in*. For Professor Firstenberg, the idea of getting someone to *buy in* to an idea or a strategy is flawed from the outset. It presupposes that the plan is already put together and needs to be sold to some group of people in order to gain their support going forward. The idea of *build in*, on the other hand is about actively involving that group of people in the development of the plan so that it is their plan and they will naturally lend their support.

Using *buy in*, it may be extremely difficult to get a company's board of directors to accept an environmental strategy that adds cost to the business and does not promise a concrete return within a reasonable time horizon. If explained properly, the board might also shy away from a strategy of *show and tell* that can potentially open the company up to risks to its reputation if an accident were to happen or an *activist* group uncovered some embarrassing practices somewhere in the firm.

If, on the other hand, time was somehow found to involve members of the board in aspects of the analysis discussed earlier, such that they were able to shape that analysis and come to their own conclusions, one might get a different result.

One approach to doing this is to establish key milestones in the analytical process in which the board can be involved. One could imagine, for example, holding a series of two or three hour workshops built around understanding the past and present, and developing scenarios for the future. If the board members were to establish the parameters for a set of scenarios in one workshop and then review the final versions of the scenarios in another, then it may be possible to build in their support for whatever strategy is finally adopted.

The task of bringing the board into such a discussion can be very difficult especially considering the demands such people have on their time and the imposition that legislation such as Sarbanes-Oxley in the United States has had on making board members delve deeply into myriad financial aspects taking time away from more strategic issues. Such involvement can, however, prove extremely valuable.

The final challenge in engaging the board on the issue of sustainability has to do with the different values and assumptions discussed in Chapter 1 and the fact that, in many cases, board members are unfamiliar with the issues surrounding environmental sustainability and receive little training about them.

Develop a Plan

Once the company has chosen to adopt a strategy, the next challenge is to put together a plan to implement that strategy. As there are a number of excellent works on strategy implementation and change management, the following will only focus on the key issues connected to a strategy for environmental sustainability.

The degree of difficulty depends on the difference between the company's starting point and the chosen strategy. It may be that, as a result of going through an exercise such as that described earlier, the board and management team decide to continue on the firm's current path and that only small adjustments need to be made.

For a firm that has a strong record on compliance, for example, the move to *wait and see* may involve nothing more than reinforcing its corporate affairs team and having regular reviews of pending legislation at a senior level. On the other hand, moving from a *low road* approach to going well beyond compliance will require much more time, energy, and investment.

With respect to the strategies outlined in Chapter 4, the key issues are the time horizon under consideration, the compelling logic of adopting the strategy, the costs and benefits involved, and what the plan means for employees and other stakeholders.

Time frame

As discussed in Chapter 4, changing corporate culture and building capabilities takes time. What is also clear is that the trend towards greater environmental scrutiny and transparency is likely to increase in most places. Putting these two trends together one might make the case for eventually doing more on the issue of environmental sustainability. The question then becomes whether to do so sooner or later.

If the adjustments to a firm's current activities are relatively modest, as in the example given here, then a time frame of one to three years may make sense. At issue will be to approve increases to head count in specific areas, consider hiring of external consultants to help with preparing sustainability reports, undertake detailed cost calculations, and so on.

If, on the other hand, the strategy is a fundamental rethink of the firm's approach, then the plan will need to span five to ten years and accommodate a number of unknowns in terms of changes to legislation, market dynamics, consumer behavior, and technological developments.

Dealing with such unknowns is fundamental in pursuing a long-term strategy and thus it becomes critical to build mechanisms to highlight key issues and track their evolution over time. This might entail setting up units in R&D, corporate affairs, sales, marketing, and operations or alternatively a central tracking unit that looks across a number of disciplines.

Compelling logic

A second critical aspect is to make crystal clear the fundamental logic of the strategy. While this point might seem self evident, there are a number of companies that have adopted a forward thinking, environmentally proactive stance, which makes it difficult to uncover the compelling business logic behind the strategy.

While such examples may simply be the adoption of a *pay for principal* approach, even that approach ought to be explained in clear terms. The high-end outdoors clothing company, Patagonia, for example, is very clear about the fact that its commitments to the environment and corporate responsibility are a direct result of the ethical point of view of the company's founder Yvon Chouinard.

Chouinard is quoted on the company's web site as saying that "Living the examined life, is a pain in the ass," and calls himself a "reluctant businessman."[1] The point is not that every company should follow Patagonia's footsteps, but that the firm is clear as to where its commitments come from. The founder of the company felt these issues were important and thus built the company around them.

As fuel cell electric and later hybrid electric vehicles appeared on the scene in the 1990s, a number of automotive manufacturers essentially adopted a *wait and see* approach. They pursued reasonable programs in R&D to be sure that they would be able to jump into these technologies when the market was considered to be ready, but held off making any sweeping commitments. One such company was Nissan, until its CEO, Carlos Ghosn, reversed his public stance on electric vehicles and embarked on the development of the Nissan Leaf, which was launched in 2010.

A rational argument can be made for adopting any one of the strategies outlined in Chapter 4, with the exception of *break the law*. If the senior management of the company chooses to deliberately not comply with the law due to a calculus that shows that potential penalties will cost less than compliance, it is inadvisable to make such a decision explicit as it could lead to prosecution. The tacit way of doing the same thing is to not put in place sufficient managerial oversight and then turn a blind eye to business practices in the field.

As mentioned in Chapter 4, while an ethically compelling argument can be made for what is called taking the *low road*, or simply complying with all relevant regulations, there can be no justification for senior management choosing to *break the law* no matter how good the business case.

Costs and benefits

Beyond the compelling logic of the strategy chosen, the plan ought to include an accurate estimate of the costs involved to achieve full compliance with environmental regulations, as well as the costs of doing more than the law requires. It should also include as full an accounting as possible of any benefits that are expected by pursuing one strategy or another.

The challenge in developing a business case in this area is that in many instances the costs will be quite clear, while some of the benefits will be much harder to quantify if such quantification is indeed possible. Cost savings due to gains in efficiency can be quantified to some degree, although energy and raw material prices do fluctuate over time, but these types of benefits are the most straightforward.

An example of such difficulty can be found in an assumption that consumers may not continue to buy a product or service if they perceive that the firm is somehow less environmentally sustainable than some if its competitors. While a business case can be made that avoiding such a risk may be worth the costs involved, determining exactly which segment of consumers are at risk and the likelihood of that risk can be very complicated.

Another example has to do with taking steps today to prepare for or hedge against environmental liabilities tomorrow. While the costs of such steps can be calculated, the benefits will only happen at some time in the future. Since it is often difficult to know if that future will happen in five, ten, or 20 years, it becomes very difficult to calculate the net present value of such an action no matter how big the future pay off or cost avoidance might be.

These difficulties again argue for deep involvement of the board. Typically, line managers can be relied upon to manage clear numbers and take decisions that support the stated financial returns of the business.

A decision that involves known costs and unknown benefits requires much more of a strategic focus and can best be taken by the CEO or the board. In the opposite case, choosing to not hedge against an uncertain future or risk serious market problems via inaction is a deep responsibility and should also be the board's decision.

Personal implications

The last key issue to address is the personal implications of adopting a specific strategy with respect to environmental sustainability. What makes the issue complex is that our relationship with the natural environment can be, like diversity, product toxicity, and a handful of other issues, much more emotionally charged than say financial or logistics strategy.

In the first place, people of all cultures and walks of life do have a relationship with the natural world. This is reflected in the foundation myths of many cultures, such Adam and Eve in the Garden of Eden, and reflected in countless works by poets, painters, photographers, and cinematographers. While this point may seem a bit mystical for a business audience, nature does have a capacity to awe and inspire and it is important to recognize that power.

Environmental interest groups certainly recognize and exploit the deep connection that many people have for the natural world and use that connection to achieve their goals. Such groups will often spend enormous amounts of energy working to sensationalize environmental issues and make them personal by setting off what Greenpeace co-founder, Patrick Moore, called "mind bombs," as discussed in Chapter 5.[2]

Such activity can also affect employees, customers, consumers, and even shareholders. It can also affect the children of different groups, who can then influence their parents' behavior in different ways.

The five strategies discussed in Chapter 4 each require different levels of personal commitment from employees and analogous actions on the part of other stakeholders.

In the *low road* and *wait and see* options, there is a deliberate choice to limit environmental behavior to whatever the law requires and, while the large majority of people will certainly be comfortable with that approach, a small segment of the population may want to do more. In this case it may be desirable for the firm to set up some kind of volunteer program to provide outlet to such energies.

These strategies also require line managers to be forthcoming with the actual state of their operations and, if there are problems, there may be incentives for them to underplay their importance or even hide them from senior management, putting the company into a tenuous legal situation. If a firm were to adapt one of the strategies that go beyond compliance, there will be an even higher level of environmental sensibility for line managers and key employees.

For a *show and tell* strategy to succeed, the key issue is to make sure that the entire operations of a firm are consistent with the messaging in its public communications. For this to work, managers and employees of all kinds must be ready to "walk the talk" and support the message in their behavior and on social media.

In order for *pay for principal* or *think ahead* to be successful, a number of key managers and operatives need to be convinced that the direction is the right one, as second guessing or endemic feet dragging can defeat such a strategy through resistance to change and inertia.

Thus implementing a comprehensive environmental strategy, at whatever level, requires thinking though the personal implication the strategy will or will not require of managers and key employees, and hence an internal and external communications strategy is critical.

Communications and Training

Once the strategy is clear at the level of the CEO and the board, the successes or failures of many strategic initiatives depend on the quality of the communications and training that managers, employees, and other stakeholders receive.

As discussed earlier, a change in a company's approach to environmental sustainability requires thinking through the personal implications for different groups of people, who may have to change the way they think or behave in order to support the strategy. While communications can help people see things in a new light, changing behavior requires training.

IESE Business School often gets involved in developing training programs for executives who are one, two, or even three levels below the CEO, in order to complement communications they have received concerning changes to the company's strategy.

What often happens in that the senior management team is deeply involved in developing such initiatives and, therefore, their support is built in to the direction, as has been discussed. Their direct reports, on the other hand, and the people further down in the hierarchy, often have not been party to such discussions, may not be aware of changes to the larger environment, and often resist such change.

Other stakeholders such as employees, unions, shareholders, and communities in which the firm operates may have even less context to work with, and thus may also not understand the logic behind the strategic direction. In many cases, people need additional information in order to understand the compelling logic of a strategy.

When dealing with environmental sustainability, many people lack a basic understanding of the technical and scientific facts involved and their opinions are often clouded by emotions and political judgments.

Thus the execution of a comprehensive communication and training effort can be critical to the success of the implementation of an environmental strategy if it involves a significant change from the current situation. Such an effort will involve different audiences, require a well thought out timetable, and involve different techniques and technologies depending on the audience and content.

Audiences

A number of different audiences should be addressed and the contents of communication materials and training programs should be customized for each group.

For relatively senior managers it is important for them to recognize why business as usual is no longer sufficient and they will need to fully understand the compelling logic of the strategy. For that, it may be necessary to take them through some of the context in which the decisions were taken, such as going through the history of the firm and its relationship to the environment, discussing the future scenarios developed, and so on.

Managers further down in the hierarchy are likely to be a little bit younger and will perhaps intuitively accept the importance of environmental sustainability; and thus communication and/or training for them may have a different focus. For such managers the key will be to clearly articulate a vision for the future in which the new strategy makes sense. The challenge for this group is that they may have more difficulty getting excited about a *wait and see* or *low road* strategy.

All managers will eventually need to feel comfortable with the message they are expected to give to their people, customers, and others outside of the firm – such as customers, journalists, government officials, and members of environmental interest groups – and thus extensive efforts are warranted to make sure they are fully in line with the strategy.

Communications and training for the rank and file is also necessary but must be done in such a way as to reinforce behavior and avoid the feeling that sustainability is the "flavor of the month" and just another speech.

Dealing with external audiences such as government officials, shareholders, and the communities in which the firm operates also requires careful messaging and, in many companies, the manager for sustainability often reports to the head of corporate communications, reflecting the importance of this facet of the role. Training can also be useful for these audiences, especially if the details of the firm's approach to environmental sustainability have a technically complex component.

Communicating the new strategy to customers and consumers is still another area, and often will be led by marketing but require deep involvement of line managers. The challenge is to carefully craft the marketing message such that it resonates with the different customer segments that the company targets while at the same time is firmly backed up by results.

A last audience, which it is worthwhile to single out, is communication and engagement with environmental interest groups, which should be undertaken by line managers and executives who have received specialized training on how to go about it. Public affairs and legal teams can support the process but it is generally preferable to have front line managers be deeply involved or even lead the process.

It is, however, important to distinguish between the different types of environmental groups, as defined in Chapter 5, as it would be one thing to engage in a round table on sustainability with an *advocate* group and another to deal with an *activist* group that is bent on eliminating an activity or *localists* who see a project as a threat to their home and children.

Conclusion

The strategic issues at play for business with respect to environmental sustainability can be extremely complex and working through them in order to come to a sound strategic response will take time, energy, and the attention of senior management.

While it is certainly tempting to maintain that doing the right thing will lead to business success, reality is much more nuanced and what is right for one company may not be right for another. Furthermore, it is very difficult to know what the "right" thing is and most firms do not have a single powerful founder, shareholder, or family of shareholders who are able to define what it means to "do the right thing" and have the ability to back their principles up by taking the long view on investments and potentially lower returns.

Due to the complexity of the strategic issues as well as the emotions and politics that dealing with the environment can provoke, there is another temptation simply not to articulate a strategic response and just delegate the issue to the relevant people in operations, public affairs, marketing, and corporate communications.

This approach is, however, very risky because a firm might end up with different parts of the organization following different strategies by default. A manager tasked with writing a sustainability report may, for example, proudly discuss a firm's environmental achievements, while an operations manager makes decisions based on cost that, while compliant with local law, may not sit well with affluent consumers in the firm's home market.

Over the last 60 years environmental sustainability has gone from an afterthought to a critical strategic issue in certain industries and in certain markets. To assume that it will all simply go away or somehow "lose steam" in the future does not seem plausible. What appears much more likely is that attention to this issue will continue to increase in waves of popular support that produce ever increasing levels of regulations and constraints on business. It is also likely that the current level of environmental attention and regulation in the United States, the European Union, and other Western countries will eventually expand to the developing world as it gets wealthier and as its own environmental problems get worse.

A strategic response to the issue, at whatever level, should not be developed as a response to some universal idea of what is right or wrong, but because the issues at play will have a material impact on the success of most, if not all, firms in the medium and long term; and dealing with such issues is the responsibility of senior management.

Notes

Introduction

1. R. Carson (1962), *Silent Spring*, Houghton Mifflin.

1 The Logic of Business: Governance and the Environment

1. G. Hardin (1968), "The tragedy of the commons," *Science*, 162, 1243–1248.
2. The Conference Board (2014), Governance Center White Paper.
3. Morck et al. (2007), *A History of Corporate Governance Around the World*, University of Chicago Press.
4. Ayan Rand (1957), *Atlas Shrugged*, Penguin.
5. A. Hax, N. Majlud (1995), *The Strategy Concept and Process: A Pragmatic Approach,* Prentice Hall.
6. P. Miller (2001), *Mission Critical Leadership*, McGraw-Hill.
7. N. Taleb (2007), *The Black Swan: The Impact of the Highly Improbable*, Random House.
8. N. Ferguson (1998), *The Pity of War*, Viking Penguin.
9. P. Polman (2014), "The remedies for capitalism," www.mckinsey.com, date accessed, March 11, 2015.
10. P. Polman (2014), "The remedies for capitalism," www.mckinsey.com, date accessed, 11 March, 2015.
11. http://longnow.org, date accessed, 14 March 2015.
12. G. Hofestede (1984), *Culture's Consequences: International Differences in Work-Related Values*, Sage.

13. R. Scruton (2012), *How To Think Seriously About The Planet*, Oxford University Press.
14. R. Scruton (2012), *How To Think Seriously About The Planet*, Oxford University Press.
15. G. Hardin (1968), "The tragedy of the commons," *Science*, 162, 1243–1248.
16. F. Reinhardt (1999), "Bringing the Environment Down to Earth," *Harvard Business Review*, July–August.
17. T. Roosevelt (1910), speech at Osawatomie, Kansas, August 31, 1910.
18. R. Carson (1962), *Silent Spring*, Houghton Mifflin.
19. D. Meadows (1979), *The Limits to Growth*, Macmillan.
20. J. Elkington (1999), *Cannibals with Forks*, Capstone.
21. D. Baron (2012), *Business and its Environment*, Prentice Hall, 7th edition.

2   Modes of Response

1. R. Carson (1962), *Silent Spring*, Houghton Mifflin.
2. M. Gladwell (2001), "The mosquito killer," *The New Yorker*, July 2, 42.
3. R. Carson (1962), *Silent Spring*, Houghton Mifflin.
4. J. Doyle (2012), "Power in the pen, Silent Spring: 1962," www.PopHistory Dig.com, date accessed, March 11, 2015.
5. C. Bryson (2006), *The Fluoride Deception*, Seven Stories Press.
6. C. Bryson (2006), *The Fluoride Deception*, Seven Stories Press.
7. P. Lagadec (1987), "From Seveso to Mexico and Bhopal: Learning to Cope with Crises," in P. Kleindorfer, H. Kunreuther (eds) *Insuring and Managing Hazardous Risks*, Springer.
8. P. Lagadec (2013), *Navigating the Unknown*, www.patricklagadec.net, date accessed, March 11, 2015.
9. J. Gottschalk (1993), *Crisis Response*, Gale Research.
10. K. Fortun (2001), *Advocacy after Bhopal*, University of Chicago Press.
11. GRI (2013), "Annual Activity Review," www.globalreporting.org, date accessed, March 11, 2015.
12. http://www.enviromedia.com/consumers-put-ads-to-greenwashing-test/, date accessed, May 2, 2015.
13. F. Reinhardt and M. Hyman (2007, revised 2009), *Global Climate Change and BP*, Harvard Business School Press.
14. D. Bello (2011), "How science stopped BP's Gulf of Mexico oil spill," *Scientific American*, April 19.
15. McKinsey interview with Kasper Rorsted, www.mckinsey.com, date accessed, June 2, 2015.

3 Strategic Issues

1. M. Porter (1996), "What is strategy?" *Harvard Business Review*, November.
2. Jason Prno (2013), "An analysis of factors leading to the establishment of a social license to operate in the mining industry," *Resources Policy*, 38–4, 577–590.
3. www.socialicense.com/definition.html, date accessed, March 11, 2015.
4. BP (2009), *Annual Report*.
5. ABC News, June 8, 2011.
6. Chichilnisky (2009), "Catastrophic risks," *Journal of Green Economics*, 3(2), 130–141.
7. Whole Foods (2014), *Annual Report* on Form 10-K.
8. Whole Foods (2012), Food Shopping Trend Tracker Survey.
9. Kano (1984), "Attractive quality and must-be quality," *Journal of the Japanese Society for Quality Control*, 14(2), 147–156.
10. J. Brower and C. Christensen (1995), "Disruptive technologies: catching the wave," *Harvard Business Review*, January.
11. J. Elkington (1998), *Cannibals with Forks*, New Society Publishers.

4 Strategic Options

1. F. Reinhardt (1999), "Bringing the environment down to earth," *Harvard Business Review*, July–August.
2. J. Shimshack (2007), "Monitoring, enforcement, & environmental compliance: understanding specific & general deterrence," EPA White Paper.
3. J. Mackey (2015), *Conscious Capitalism*, Harvard Business Review Press.
4. P. Wack (1985), "Shooting the rapids," *Harvard Business Review*, November–December.

5 Environmental Interest Groups

1. M. McCloskey (2012), *In the Thick of It: My Life in the Sierra Club*, Island Press.
2. P. Moore (2013), *Confessions of a Greenpeace Dropout: The Making of a Sensible Environmentalist*, Beatty Street Publishing.
3. www.stopthesethings.com/about/, date accessed, March 11, 2015.
4. www.wind-watch.org/allies.php, date accessed, March 11, 2015.
5. J. Lovelock (2007), *The Revenge of Gaia: Why the Earth is Fighting Back and How We Can Still Save Humanity*, Penguin.

6. R. Scruton (2012), *How To Think Seriously About The Planet*, Oxford University Press.
7. Environment 360, http://e360.yale.edu/, date accessed, December 15, 2014.

6 Industry Examples

1. IEA (2014), "Key world energy statistics."
2. www.iea.org, date accessed, February 15, 2015.
3. M. Melosi (2005), "The automobile and the environment in American history," *Automobile in American Life and Society*, www.autolife.umd.umich.edu, date accessed, January 15, 2015.
4. http://archive.fortune.com/galleries/2010/fortune/1005/gallery.expensive_oil_spills.fortune/2.html, accessed May 26 2015.
5. OCIMF (2003), "Double hull tankers – are they the answer?"
6. BP (2014), *Sustainability Report*.
7. E. Crooks (2014), "Oil majors' R&D into conventional and renewable energy at Risk," *Financial Times*, September 25.
8. E. Crooks (2014), "Oil majors' R&D into Conventional and Renewable Energy at risk," *Financial Times*, September 25.
9. Shell Oil (2008), "Brent Spar Dossier," www.shell.com, date accessed, March 12, 2015.
10. www.greenpeace.org, date accessed, March 10, 2015.
11. www.oica.net, date accessed, February 10, 2015.
12. www.oica.net, date accessed, February 10, 2015.
13. D. Gordon, D. Sperling (2009), *Two Billion Cars*, Oxford University Press.
14. R. Nader (1965), *Unsafe at Any Speed*, Grossman Publishers.
15. Pew Environment (2011), "History of fuel economy."
16. Associated Press (2014), "Tesla Selects Nevada for Battery Plant," *Salt Lake Tribune*, January 3.
17. C. Knud-Hansen (1994), "Historical Perspective of the Phosphate Detergent Conflict," Conflict Research Forum, Working Paper 94–95.
18. K. Booman, R. Sedlak (1984), "Detergent research at SDA," Presented at the 57th annual convention of The Soap and Detergent Association, Boca Raton, FL, January 28.
19. C. Knud-Hansen (1994), "Historical perspective of the phosphate detergent conflict," Conflict Research Forum, Working Paper 94–95.
20. "Which Soda Packaging Has the Biggest Carbon Footprint?" www.earth911.com, date accessed, February 20, 2015.
21. M. Cutifani (2013), "A critical imperative – innovation and a sustainable future," World Mining Congress, Montreal, Canada, July 2.

22. BHP Billiton (2014), 2014 *Sustainability Report*, 27.
23. Boliden (1998), 1998 *Annual Report*, 7.
24. M. Mills (2013), "The cloud begins with coal," www.tech-pundit.com, date accessed March 14, 2015.
25. GeSI (2012), *SMARTer 2020*, www.gesi.org, date accessed, March 14, 2015.
26. http://www.google.com/green, date accessed, May 26, 2015.
27. IAE (2014), "More data, less energy," www.iea.org, date accessed, March 14, 2015.
28. Greenpeace (2014), "Clicking clean," www.greenpeace.org, date accessed, March 14, 2015.
29. GeSI (2012), *SMARTer 2020*, www.gesi.org, date accessed, March 14, 2015.
30. Apple (2014), *Environmental Responsibility Report*, 18.
31. Samsung (2014), *Sustainability Report*, 117.
32. Transparency Market Research (2013), "Electronic recycling market."
33. GeSI (2012), *SMARTer 2020*, www.gesi.org, date accessed, March 14, 2015.

7   Regional Differences

1. D. Stern (2004), "The rise and fall of the Environmental Kuznets Curve," *World Development*, 32–38, 1419–1439.
2. U.S. Census Bureau (2013), "Income and poverty in the United States."
3. P. Krugman (2014), "On inequality denial," *The New York Times*, January 6.
4. Shelton Digital (2014), *Eco Pulse 2014*.
5. Lachapelle et al. (2012), "Public attitudes toward climate science and climate policy in federal systems: Canada and the United States compared," *Review of Policy Research*, 29–23, 334–357.
6. www.eia.gov, date accessed, February 15, 2014.
7. http://ec.europa.eu/eurostat/statistics, date accessed, February 15, 2014.
8. R. Scruton (2012), *How To Think Seriously About The Planet*, Oxford University Press.
9. European Union (2011), "Attitudes of European citizens towards the environment," EB75.2.
10. D. Rothkopf (2013), *Power, Inc.: The Epic Rivalry between Big Business and Government and the Reckoning That Lies Ahead,* Farrar, Straus and Giroux.
11. C. Simons (2013), *The Devouring Dragon: How China's Rise Threatens Our Natural World*, St. Martin's Press.
12. C. Simons (2013), *The Devouring Dragon: How China's Rise Threatens Our Natural World*, St. Martin's Press.

13. www.worldometers.info, date accessed, February 20, 2014.
14. H. Sanderson, M. Forsythe (2013), *China's Superbank: Debt, Oil and Influence – How China Development Bank is Rewriting the Rules of Finance*, Bloomberg Press.
15. B. Zhang, C. Cao (2015), "Four gaps in China's new environmental law," *Nature*, 517, 433.
16. E. Grumbine (2013), *Environment 360*, "China at the crossroads," date accessed, January 15, 2015.
17. B. Zhang, C. Cao (2015), "Four gaps in China's new environmental law," *Nature*, 517, 433.
18. www.globalcarbonatlas.org, date accessed, February 10, 2014.
19. N. Madhaven et al. (2013), "Paucity amidst plenty," *Business Today*, India, December 22.
20. www.worldometers.info, date accessed, February 20, 2014.
21. E. Broughton (2005), "The Bhopal disaster and its aftermath: A review," *Environmental Health*, 4, 6.
22. S. Bengali (2015), "India cracks down on greenpeace, other environmental groups," *LA Times*, January 1.
23. B. Simons (2012), "Africa's fabulous mineral wealth that isn't all there," www.africanarguments.org, date accessed, March 14, 2015.
24. Energy Intelligence (2011), "Africa's oil and gas potential."
25. KPMG (2013), "Oil and gas in Africa."
26. J. Randers (2012), *2052-A Global Forecast for the Next Forty Years*, Chelsea Green Publishing.
27. E. Amechi (2010), "Linking environmental protection and poverty reduction in Africa: An analysis of the regional legal responses to environmental protection," *Law, Environment and Development Journal*, 6–2, 112–129.

8 What to Do?

1. www.patagonia.com, date accessed, February 10, 2015.
2. P. Moore (2013), *Confessions of a Greenpeace Dropout: The Making of a Sensible Environmentalist*, Beatty Street Publishing.

Index

A

activists   39–40, 121–4, 131
advocates   113, 128–30, 131
Africa   190–6
African Conservation Tillage Network   193
African Wildlife   193
Air pollution   34, 47, 133, 142–3, 180, 187
Amazon region   83, 123
Amazon company   162
Amchitka island   122
Amnesty International   118
Anderson, Warren   51
Anglo American   155, 158
Apple   162–5
Arctic   135, 197–8

B

B corporations   104
Baotou   160
Barings Bank   70
Baron, David   37–8
Bergin, Patrick   194
Berry, Phil   117
Bhopal   36, 49–52, 70–1, 83, 90, 96, 101, 187
BHP Billiton   156
Boliden   157

bottles   84, 150–3
BPA   152–3
Branson, Richard   90, 104, 106–7
British Petroleum   54–6, 59, 61–2, 68, 75–6, 136–8
Brower, David   116–17, 121
Browne, John   54–6, 61–2, 68, 75
Browning, Jackson   49–50, 52
Brune, Michael   118

C

CAFE   142
cans   151–2
Carson, Rachel   34, 43–5
catalytic converter   143
change management   108, 208
Chernobyl   36
Chichilnisky, Graciela   71
China   9, 145, 163, 174, 179–84, 189, 196, 197–8
China Labor Watch   163
chlorofluorocarbons (CFCs)   36, 81
Chouinard, Yvon   104, 210
Christensen, Clayton   79
Citigroup   83
Climate change   36, 55
Clinton Climate Initiative   60
clock of the long now   21–2
Coal India   185

Coca-Cola Company   153
Colby, William   115
coltan   174
compact fluorescent lamps   80
conservationists   37, 67, 113, 119–21,
   131–2
consumer behavior   72–8, 85, 166,
   179, 204
Cooney, Jim   66
Copenhagen Consensus   16
Corporate affairs   65, 131
corporate governance   40, 61–2,
   205–8
corporate social responsibility
   (CSR)   55, 66–9
Cousteau, Jacques   34
cover up   41, 46–9, 61
crisis management   42, 49–53, 61
Cutifani, Mark   155

D
DDT   34–5, 43–5, 61, 117
De Haven, Hugh   141
Deepwater Horizon   55–6, 68,
   136, 166
Diablo Canyon   121
Doer, John   104
Donaña   157
Donora   34, 47–9, 61
Doublehulltankers   136
Dudley, Robert   68
Dutschke, Rudi   39

E
Earth Day   35
electric cars   75, 80, 144–5, 146–7
Elkington, John   36
Emerson, Ralph Waldo   32, 119
Empire State Building   60
Environmental Defense Fund   93, 123
environmental Kuznets curve   169, 182

Environmental Protection Agency
   (EPA)   125, 143
Europe and theEuropean Union   33,
   82, 149, 150, 152, 174–9, 196
Exxon Mobile   137
Exxon Valdez   135, 166

F
Facebook   161–2, 165
Ferguson, Niall   20
Firstenberg, Iris   207
flaring (natural gas)   137
fluoride   47–8, 61
Ford, Henry   12
Foxconn   163
Friends of the Earth   117, 123
Fukushima   70–1

G
Gamesa   59–62
Ghosn, Carlos   210
Gibbs, Lois   125
Global Climate Coalition   55, 137
Global Reporting Initiative   53,
   153, 159
Globalization   81–4, 85, 167, 193
Google   161–2, 165
Gore, Al   104
green dot   176
green party   177
Greenpeace   122–4, 135, 138, 139–40,
   154, 162, 198
greenwashing   53–4, 56, 74, 101, 201
group think   47
Grumbine, Edward   182

H
Hayward, Tony   55, 56, 68
Hardin, Garret   6, 28–9
Henkel   9, 57–9, 62, 89–90, 149,
   154, 167

Hewlett Packard (HP)   12, 19
Hill, Julia (Butterfly)   127
Home Depot   11
hydraulic fracturing (fracking)   126,
    135, 177

I
India   185–90
Intergovernmental Panel on
Climate Change (IPCC)   36, 55
International Energy Agency
    36, 55
International Marine Forum
    136–7

J
Japan Tobacco International (JTI)
    201
Johnson & Johnson   153

K
Kano, Noriaki   76–8, 142
Kennedy, John F.   45
Keystone XL   118, 173
kitkat   68–9, 123, 203
Kroko, Pano   197–8
Krugman, Paul   171
Kyotoprotocol   16, 36–7, 204

L
deLabouchere, Pierre   201
Lagadec, Patrick   49–53
LaMantia, Charlie   25
LED Lighting   80
Levine, Mark   47
License to Operate   66–9
Lomborg, Bjorn   15, 16–17
Love canal   35–6, 125
Lovelock, James   81, 126
Lovins, Amory   129

M
Mackey, John   73, 105
malaria   34, 44–5, 61
Mather, Stephen   115
McCloskey, Michael   117–18
McDonalds   93
Mercury poisoning   34
Miller, Paddy   19
Minas-Rio   158–9
Minimata disease   34
Mittal, Lakshmi   12
Modi, Narendra   187
Moore, Patrick   122, 212
Muir, John   32, 37, 114–15
Muller, Paul   44
Musk, Elon   146

N
Nader, Ralph   141
National Trust   33
Nelson, Gaylord   35
Nestlé   68–9, 82, 123, 148, 154,
    203
Niktin, Alexander   118
Not in my backyard (NIMBY)   127
NTA (sodiumnitrilotriacetate)   149
nuclear power   22, 27, 36, 70, 84, 113,
    118, 121, 131, 184

O
Obama, Barak   68
oikophilia   127, 175
oil and gas   133, 134–40

P
Palm oil   68–9, 82, 94, 154, 203
Patagonia   106, 210
path dependency   200
Pegatron   163
PET   150, 152

phosphates   75, 148-9, 166-7, 173
Pinchot, Gifford   115
Polman, Paul   20-1, 22
Porter, Michael   38
Poza Rica   34
precautionary principal   28, 44,
    124, 149
Prestige   136
Proctor& Gamble   148-9
prospect theory   46

R

Rain ForestAction Network   83
Rand, Ayn   11, 14
Reinhard, Forest   29, 91
renaissancedam   191
Rio summit   28
risk   26-8, 40, 51, 63, 70-2, 84-5,
    200, 206, 211-12
robberbarons   12
Rocky Mountain Institute
    (RMI)   129-30
Roosevelt, Theodore   32, 37, 115
Rorsted, Kasper   58

S

Samsung   162-5
Sandoz   36
Sarbanes-Oxley   25, 208
scenario planning   23-4, 71, 108, 109,
    203-4
Scruton, Roger   26, 28, 119,
    127, 175
Shell   23, 138, 139-40, 167, 193
Sierra Club   32, 114-19, 120, 121,
    127, 188
Silent Spring   1, 34, 43-5
Simmons, Craig   180
Simons, Bright   190-1
Singh, Manmohan   186

Siri, William   121
South North Water Transfer
    Project   180
Stop These Things   126
strategic planning   17-18, 23
Sullenberger, C.B.   52
summer of love   35
sustainability reporting   78

T

tantalum   163, 190
Tata, Ratan   12
Technological innovation   78-81
Tesla Motors   80, 145, 146-7
Tetra pak   152
Thomson, Ian   67
Thoreau, Henry David   32, 119
time value of money   15
tobacco industry   13-14, 201
TorreyCanyon   135, 136
Toyota   144, 146
tragedy of the commons   6, 28
triple bottom line   25
Tuerff, Kevin   54
Tylenol   153, 166

U

U.S. Forest Service   117
U.S. Steel   34, 47-9, 61
Unilever   94
Union Carbide   187
United Nation's Global Compact   21,
    25, 58
United States   82, 170-4
Unsafe at Any Speed   141

V

Videla, Pedro   168
Virgin   90, 106-7
Volvo   141

W

Wack, Pierre   49–53, 61, 70, 83, 90, 109
Watts, James   118
WholeFoods   73–4, 105
willingness to pay   72, 76, 137

X

Xiaoping, Deng   181

Y

Yellowstone   32
Yosemite   32, 114–15, 119

Z

zeolith A   149

Printed and bound in Great Britain by
CPI Group (UK) Ltd, Croydon, CR0 4YY